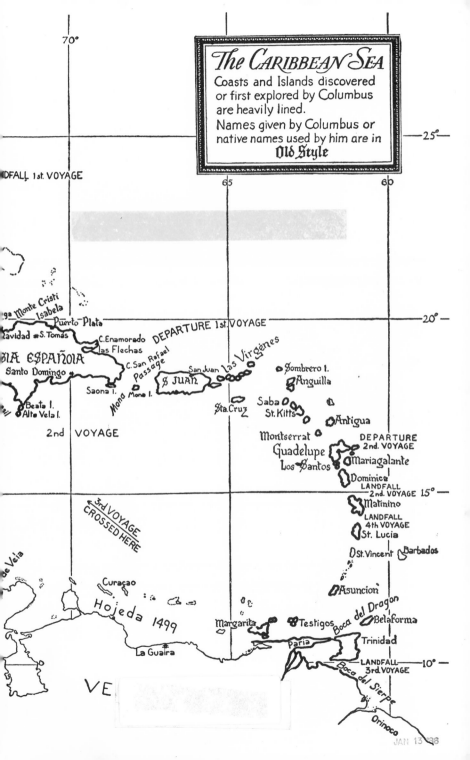

The Caribbean Sea

Coasts and Islands discovered or first explored by Columbus are heavily lined.

Names given by Columbus or native names used by him are in **Old Style**

CHRISTOPHER COLUMBUS, MARINER

Christopher Columbus, Mariner

BY

SAMUEL ELIOT MORISON

Maps by Erwin Raisz

An Atlantic Monthly Press Book

LITTLE, BROWN AND COMPANY

BOSTON   TORONTO

LIBRARY OF CONGRESS CATALOG CARD NO. 55–8096

Sixteenth Printing

ATLANTIC–LITTLE, BROWN BOOKS
ARE PUBLISHED BY
LITTLE, BROWN AND COMPANY
IN ASSOCIATION WITH
THE ATLANTIC MONTHLY PRESS

BP

*Published simultaneously in Canada
by Little, Brown & Company (Canada) Limited*

PRINTED IN THE UNITED STATES OF AMERICA

To my Dearest,
PRISCILLA BARTON MORISON,
this, the first book written at our
"Good Hope,"
is affectionately dedicated.

Preface

THE LIFE AND VOYAGES of Christopher Columbus have been a hobby of mine for almost fifty years. After reading almost everything on the subject that was in print, I reached the conclusion that what Columbus wanted was a sailor biographer, one who knew ships and sailing and who had visited, under sail, the islands and mainland that he discovered. A preliminary reconnaissance of the Windward and Leeward Islands in the yawl *Ptarmigan*, in the winter of 1937–1938, acted on me like a fresh wind on a becalmed ship; it pulled me out of the calms and shoals of unprofitable speculation into the clear blue water of practical experience. So, with the help of Mr. Paul Hammond, I organized the Harvard Columbus Expedition consisting of the barkentine *Capitana* and ketch *Mary Otis* (Captain William D. Stevens), which in 1939–1940 crossed the Atlantic from New England to Lisbon via the Azores, visited Huelva, Palos, Cadiz, Porto Santo, Madeira, and the Grand Canary, and jumped off from Gomera to follow as closely as possible the track of Columbus's Third Voyage. We made the same landfall that he did on Trinidad, followed his course along the Gulf of Paria, ascertaining where he first landed on the continent and where he took possession, and then sailed into the Caribbean by the Bocas, picked up the route of Columbus's Fourth Voyage at the Gulf of Darien, and followed it along the coast of the Republic of Panama to Costa Rica, and then to Jamaica. In the summer of 1940 Captain Stevens took me in *Mary Otis* (the *Niña* of our expedition) through the Bahamas and along all the coasts and cays of Cuba that Columbus explored on his First and Second Voyages. On other occasions I flew to Hispaniola and followed Columbus's routes about that island by car, on foot and in a small vessel of the Garde d'Haiti.

The result of these voyages, applied to years of research in the documents and printed sources of the time, appeared in 1942 as *Admiral of the Ocean Sea: A Life of Christopher Columbus*, a two-volume edition with copious notes, and a somewhat shortened one-volume edition without notes. The latter was awarded the Pulitzer Prize for Biography that year. The former has been translated into Spanish and German.

In this book, which I have entitled *Christopher Columbus, Mariner*, I have rewritten the entire story of the Discoverer's life and voyages, in the hope of reaching a wider public, and I have added a fresh translation of Columbus's own Letter on his First Voyage. My account is a straightforward narrative, giving my own conclusions on the numerous controversial points in the Admiral's career. If any reader wishes to know my sources or reasons for these statements, he is referred to my two-volume biography. My point of view is still that of a sailor, relating the achievements of him whom I believe to have been one of the greatest mariners, if not the very greatest, of all time.

SAMUEL ELIOT MORISON

"Good Hope"
Northeast Harbor, Maine
September, 1954

Contents

List of Maps, Charts and Illustrations

CHRISTOPHER COLUMBUS, MARINER

Christopher Goes to Sea

CHRISTOPHER COLUMBUS, Discoverer of the New World, was first and foremost a sailor. Born and raised in Genoa, one of the oldest European seafaring communities, as a youth he made several voyages in the Mediterranean, where the greatest mariners of antiquity were bred. At the age of twenty-four, by a lucky chance he was thrown into Lisbon, center of European oceanic enterprise; and there, while employed partly in making charts and partly on long voyages under the Portuguese flag, he conceived the great enterprise that few but a sailor would have planned, and none but a sailor could have executed. That enterprise was simply to reach "The Indies" — Eastern Asia — by sailing west. It took him about ten years to obtain support for this idea, and he never did execute it, because a vast continent stood in the way. America was discovered by Columbus purely by accident and was named for a man who had nothing to do with it; we now honor Columbus for doing something that he never intended to do, and never knew what he had done. Yet we are right in so honoring him, because no other sailor had the persistence, the knowledge and the sheer guts to sail thousands of miles into the unknown ocean until he found land.

This was the most spectacular and most far-reaching geographical discovery in recorded human history. Moreover, apart from the magnitude of his achievement, Columbus was a highly interesting character. Born at the crossroads between the Middle Ages and the Renaissance, he showed the qualities of both eras. He had the firm religious faith, the a-priori reasoning and the close communion with the Unseen typical of the early Christian centuries. Yet he also had the scientific curiosity, the zest for life, the feeling for beauty and the striving for novelty that we associate with the advancement of learning. And he was one of the greatest seamen of all time.

The story starts in Genoa with the Discoverer's parents: Domenico Colombo, a wool weaver as his father had been before him, and his wife Susanna, a weaver's daughter. Domenico belonged to the middle class of Genoa. He was a member of the local wool-weavers' gild, the medieval equivalent of a trade union. He owned his own looms and employed journeymen to help him produce woolen cloth. Popular in his community, he was elected to small offices in the gild, but his wife and family found him a somewhat poor provider. He was the kind of father whom boys love, who would shut up shop on a fine day and take them fishing. So the good canceled out the bad, and Christopher named the oldest city in the New World, Santo Domingo, after his father's patron saint.

At some time between August and October 1451, the exact day is unknown, Susanna Colombo gave birth to a son who was named Cristoforo. Why his parents chose this name we do not know, but in so doing they furthered the natural bent of the boy's mind. Saint Christopher was a tall, stout pagan who yearned to know Christ but could not seem to do anything about it. He dwelt on the bank of a river in Asia Minor where there was a dangerous ford, and by reason of his great stature and strength helped many a traveler to cross. One day when he was asleep in his cabin he heard a Child's voice cry out, "Christopher! Come and set me across the river!" So out he came, staff in hand, and took the Infant on his shoulders. As he waded across, the Child's weight so increased that it was all he could do to keep from stumbling and falling, but he reached the other bank safely. "Well now, my lad," said he, "thou hast put me in great danger, for thy burden waxed so great that had I borne the whole world on my back it could have weighed no more than thee!" To which the Child replied, "Marvel not, for thou hast borne upon thy back the whole world and Him who created it. I am the Child whom thou servest in doing good to mankind. Plant thy staff near yonder cabin, and tomorrow it shall put forth flowers and fruit — proof that I am indeed thy Lord and Saviour." Christopher did as he was bid, and sure enough, next morning, his staff had become a beautiful date palm.

So from that day forth Christopher has been the patron saint of all who travel by land, sea or air. In his name Christopher Columbus saw a sign that he was destined to bring Christ across the sea to men who knew Him not. Indeed, the oldest known map of the New World, dated A.D. 1500, dedicated to Columbus by his shipmate Juan de la Cosa, is ornamented by a vignette of Saint Christopher carrying the Infant Jesus on his shoulders.

The Colombo family were respectable, but rather happy-go-lucky. Domenico was always on the move, though he never went farther than Savona, a few miles from Genoa, and he was always taking on new "lines" besides weaving, and losing money on them. After Christopher the eldest — at least of those who survived infancy — he had a boy who died young, a girl who married a neighboring cheesemonger, Bartholomew who became the Discoverer's partner, shipmate and executive; and Giacomo, Christopher's junior by seventeen years, who also accompanied him to the New World and is always known by the Spanish equivalent, Diego, of his first name. Domenico's brother Antonio also had a large family, and one of his sons, Giannetto (Johnny), commanded a caravel on the Third Voyage. Family feeling was very strong among the Genoese, as among the Corsicans (who then belonged to the same Republic), and just as Napoleon Bonaparte found thrones or titles for his entire family, so Christopher Columbus, a stranger in Spain, felt he could best trust his brothers and kindred.[1]

The little we know about the Discoverer's childhood and early youth can be quickly told. He had very little formal schooling, spoke the Genoese dialect, which was almost unintelligible to other Italians, and never learned to read and write until he went to Portugal. As everyone who described him in later life said that he had a long face, an aquiline nose, ruddy complexion and red hair, we can picture him as a little, freckled-faced redhead with blue eyes. One imagines that he was a dreamy little boy and very religious for one of his age, and he must have disliked working in his father's loom shed, as he took every opportunity to go to sea.

There were plenty of opportunities in that seafaring community. Almost all the traffic along the Ligurian coast was sea-borne. And everyone who had no other job, besides many who did, went fishing. Big carracks and galleons were built in the harbor; there were boat yards in every cove along the shore; and the ships of the Republic traded with all parts of the Mediterranean and with Northern Europe.

In later life Columbus said that he first went to sea in 1461 when he was ten years old. Probably his seafaring at that age did not amount to much; maybe his father let him sail with a neighbor to Portofino to load dried fish, or even over to Corsica, which would have seemed like a foreign voyage to a little boy. What sailor can

[1] The name Colombo means "dove." The English-speaking peoples have always called the Discoverer, Columbus, probably because they first read about him in the Latin history of Peter Martyr. When Columbus went to Portugal, he was called Colom; in Spain he first called himself Coloma and then changed to Colón, by which he is always known in Spanish-speaking lands. The French call him Christophe Colomb, but the Italians still refer to him by the name he was christened, Cristoforo Colombo.

forget his first cruise? Every incident, every turn of wind, every vessel or person you meet stays in your memory for years. What pride and joy to be given the tiller while the skipper goes below and the mate snoozes on the sunny side of the deck! What a thrill to sight five mountains above the horizon, to watch them rise, spread out and merge into one as you approach! Then, to go ashore, to swap your jackknife for a curiosity, to see the island gradually sink below the horizon on the homeward passage, and to swagger ashore feeling you are a real old salt! Such things a sailor never forgets.

Exactly when Christopher decided to quit the weaving trade and make the sea his profession we do not know. Facts about his early life are few; one has to piece together incidents that he or his friends remembered after he became famous, or which were recorded in a notary's office because of some litigation. It is probable that for a period of about eight years, between ages fifteen and twenty-three, Christopher made several long voyages in the Mediterranean but spent most of his time ashore helping his father. When he was nineteen, he served in a Genoese ship chartered by King René II of Anjou as part of his war fleet in a brief brawl with the King of Aragon. Christopher also made at least one voyage to Chios in the Aegean, in a ship owned by Genoese merchants, who had the monopoly of trade with that island.

In May 1476, in his twenty-fifth year, came the adventure that changed the course of Christopher's life. Genoa organized an armed convoy to carry a valuable cargo to Northern Europe, and in this convoy Christopher sailed as seaman in a Flemish vessel named *Bechalla*. On August 13, when it had passed the Strait of Gibraltar and was off the southern coast of Portugal, the fleet was attacked by a French task force. The battle raged all day, and by nightfall three Genoese ships and four of the enemy's had gone down. *Bechalla* was one of the casualties. Christopher, though wounded, managed to grasp a floating sweep and, by alternately kicking it ahead and resting on it, reached the shore six miles distant. The people of Lagos, near which he landed, treated him kindly, and on learning that his younger brother Bartholomew was living at Lisbon, sent him thither as soon as he could travel.

That was one of the best things that could have happened to Christopher Columbus.

CHAPTER II

Sailing for Portugal

PORTUGAL was then the liveliest and most progressive country in Europe, and Lisbon the center for exploration and discovery. Almost half a century earlier the Infante Dom Henrique, the Portuguese prince whom we call Henry the Navigator, had set up a combined hydrographic and marine intelligence office at Cape St. Vincent, which attracted ambitious seamen from all over the Mediterranean. He subsidized voyages out into the Atlantic and down along the west coast of Africa. His captains discovered the seven islands of the Azores, one third of the way to America; the Portuguese colonized not only the Azores but the Madeira group which had been discovered earlier, and the Cape Verde Islands off Africa. That "dark continent" was Prince Henry's particular interest. Every few years his captains made a new farthest south along the west coast, and by the time Columbus reached Lisbon, they had crossed the Gulf of Guinea. Fleets of lateen-rigged caravels, fast and weatherly little vessels specially designed for the African trade, set forth from Lisbon every spring carrying cargoes of red cloth, glass beads, hawks' bells and horses, and every fall returned with rich cargoes of ivory, gold dust, Malagueta pepper and Negro slaves. Lisbon is an ocean-facing city; from her quays there is no long and tedious sail to blue water. At a time when the Levantine commerce of Genoa was being taken away by the Venetians and Turks, Lisbon was up-and-coming, pioneering trade routes around the great circle from

Iceland through the Azores to the Gold Coast. Enterprising merchants and seamen of all countries, including those of Genoa, flocked to Lisbon to share the wealth. And the Portuguese crown deliberately fostered voyages to discover new islands and find a way to India around Africa.

Lisbon, moreover, was a learned city where it was easy for a newcomer like Columbus to learn Latin and modern languages, and to acquire books that increased his knowledge of the world. Bartholomew, who had already joined the Genoese community there, was employed in one of the chart-making establishments, where he got a job for Christopher, and before long the Columbus brothers had a thriving chart business of their own. That put them in close touch with master mariners and the like, for all charts at that time were based on information and rough sketches that seamen brought home. The two brothers would manage to be on hand whenever a ship returned from Africa or the Western Islands to invite the master or pilot to dine or drink with them, and would extract from him all the data they could for correcting their charts of known countries or extending those of the African coast. It may well be that in one of these conferences a grizzled captain, looking at a chart of the known world, remarked, "I'm sick of sailing along the fever-stricken Guinea coast, chaffering with local chiefs for a cargo of blackamoors; why can't we sail due west beyond the Azores, till we hit the Golden East, and make a real killing?"

Why not, indeed? People had been talking of doing that since the days of the Roman Empire, but nobody had tried it within the memory of man. The ocean was reputed too broad, winds too uncertain; the ships could not carry enough cargo to feed their crews for several months, and the sailors themselves had acquired deep respect for that dark and turbulent waste, the North Atlantic, and would not engage in such an enterprise. That it was theoretically

possible to reach the Orient by sailing west every educated man
would admit, since every educated man knew the earth to be a
sphere, but nobody had done anything to test the theory. In 1476,
when Columbus reached Lisbon, the proposition of sailing west
to reach the Orient was at about the same stage as man-made
flight in 1900 — theoretically possible but full of practical difficulties. Habit, custom and superstition were against it, too: "Man
should not tempt the Almighty by seeking unknown depths of the
ocean," in 1476; "Man was made for the earth, not the sky," in
1900. Most sensible people admitted that a voyage west to China
could be made, and a few said it should be done, but nobody cared
to try, until that young Genoese Cristoforo Colombo began
pestering people to finance his project.

Exactly when and how he got the idea we do not know. It
may have been put to him, as we suggest, by a shipmaster impatient of the dangers and disappointments of the Guinea trade. It
may have come to him in a rush of religious emotion at Mass,
when he heard Psalm 19, "The Heavens declare the Glory of
God"; for a Genoa compatriot remarked that Christopher fulfilled the prophecy of the fourth verse, "And their words unto the
ends of the world." He may have read that prophecy of Seneca
in the *Medea*, "A time will come when the chains of the Ocean
will fall apart, and a vast continent be revealed; when a pilot will
discover new worlds and Thule no longer be the ultimate." That
prophecy, too, was fulfilled by him, as his son Ferdinand duly
noted in his copy of Seneca. We do not know how Columbus
came by the idea of sailing west to reach the East, but once he had
it, that was the truth for him; he was the sort of man in whom
action is the complement of a dream. He *knew* the truth, but he
could not rest until it was proved, until the word became flesh.
And, let us admit, his combination of creative imagination with
obstinate assurance, his impatience with all who were slow to be

convinced and contempt for those who withstood him, made Columbus a fool in the eyes of some men and a bore to most. Like the pioneers of aviation, he was considered a little touched in the head: one who would fly in the face of God. And the worst of it was that he had to persuade stupid people in high places that his Enterprise of the Indies, as he called it, was plausible, because he wanted money, men and equipment to carry it out.

More maritime experience than that of foremast hand and apprentice chartmaker was needed before he could hope to convince anyone. And that he obtained, under the Portuguese flag. In the fall of the same year that he arrived in Lisbon, he shipped on one of the Portuguese vessels in the "Atlantic Corridor" trade — exchanging wool, dried fish and wine between Iceland, Ireland, the Azores and Lisbon. His vessel called at Galway, where, in later years, he recalled having seen two dead people in a drifting boat, of such extraordinary appearance that the Irish said they must be Chinese; probably they were Finns who had left a sinking ship. The master of the vessel in which Columbus sailed, in February 1477 went exploring to the north of Iceland for a hundred leagues before returning to Portugal, so Columbus could boast that he had sailed to the edge of the Arctic Circle.

The following year, when Columbus was twenty-seven years old, the Genoese firm under which he had earlier sailed to Chios employed him to purchase a quantity of sugar at Madeira and carry it to Genoa. They neglected, however, to supply him with money to pay for it, and the merchants of Funchal refused to deliver on credit, so Columbus reached Genoa without the sugar. There was a lawsuit, and Christopher made a deposition about the case at Genoa in the summer of 1479. That was probably his last visit to his native place. But "that noble and powerful city by the sea," as he called it in his will, was ever close to his heart, and he hoped to be able from his property to maintain a home there forever for his descendants. He never became naturalized in any other country, and he appointed the Bank of St. George at Genoa executor of his will.

Upon his return to Lisbon from Genoa, Christopher married Dona Felipa Perestrello e Moniz, scion of one of the first families of Portugal, daughter of Bartholomew Perestrello, hereditary captain of Porto Santo in the Madeira group, and granddaughter to Gil Moniz, a knight companion of Prince Henry. The young couple lived for a time in Lisbon with Dona Felipa's mother, who broke out her late husband's logbooks and charts for the benefit of her son-in-law. Later they settled in Porto Santo, where Dona Felipa's brother was governor, and there their only child, Diego, later known as Don Diego Colón, Second Admiral and Viceroy of the Indies, was born. About the year 1482 they moved to Funchal in Madeira, and while there Columbus made one and probably two voyages to São Jorge da Mina, the fortified trading post which the Portuguese crown had established on the Gold Coast. And on one of these voyages he was in command.

There is evidence, too, that he knew the Azores fairly well. Although it may not be true that on the northern point of Corvo he saw a natural rock statue of a horseman pointing west, the rock formations there are so fantastic that it requires no great imagination to see such figures. We, in 1939, made out there an armed and vizored crusader with folded arms, gazing toward Newfoundland, and hoped it did not mean Adolf Hitler!

Christopher Columbus, now aged thirty-one or -two, had "arrived," according to the standards of his day. He was a master mariner in the Portuguese merchant service, then the finest and most far-ranging merchant marine in the world. He had sailed from above the Arctic Circle almost to the Equator, and from the Eastern Aegean to the outer Azores. He had learned all of practical navigation that could be acquired by entering ships "through the hawse hole" and working up to the captain's cabin. He could make charts and figure latitude from the North Star. Besides, he was an avid reader of books on geography and cosmography. He was connected by marriage with two important families of Portugal. He had business connections with a leading merchant-banker house of Genoa. Columbus had only to continue in this career, persevere in the African trade with its many opportunities to make something on the side, and retire after a few years, a rich man. Or the King might give him one of the royal caravels to explore the African coast, as Diego Cão was doing in 1482–1483; and Cão, for discovering a new farthest south on the African coast, was knighted and ennobled in 1484.

But Christopher had other ideas and a vaster ambition. His mind was seething with the notion of sailing west to the Orient, acquiring wealth beyond the dreams of avarice, and glory exceeding that of any earlier mariner.

CHAPTER III

A Great Enterprise Is Born

THE INDIES, meaning most of Eastern Asia — India, Burma, China, Japan, the Moluccas and Indonesia — cast a spell over European imagination in the fifteenth century. These were lands of vast wealth in gold, silver and precious stones, in silk and fine cotton, in spices, drugs and perfumes, which in small quantities were taken by caravans across Asia to Constantinople or to Levantine ports, thence distributed through Europe by ship, wagon and pack train. The cost of handling by so many middlemen and over such long and complicated routes made the prices of Oriental goods to the European consumer exorbitant; yet the increase of wealth and luxury in European cities kept the demand far ahead of the supply. That is why the kings of Portugal made repeated attempts to get around Africa to India, where Oriental products could be purchased cheap. Columbus decided that the African route was the hard way to the Indies; he proposed to find a bold but easy way, due west by sea.

And there were other reasons for seeking a new and easy contact with the Far East, which appealed to so religious a man as Columbus, and still more to the churchmen who held many of the highest posts in European governments. It was a matter of intense mortification to them that the Crusades had failed, that Christians had been forced to evacuate the Holy Land, and that the Holy Sepulchre at Jerusalem, and the birthplace of Our Lord, were now controlled by infidel Turks. Somewhere in the Orient, it was believed, existed a powerful Christian state ruled by a monarch known as Prester John. The substance behind this legend was the Kingdom of Ethiopia, over which Haile Selassie's ancestors then ruled. If only contact could be made and an alliance concluded with Prester John, who was rumored to have enormous wealth and a big army, the Christian hosts might recover the Holy Land and send the Turks reeling back to Central Asia.

European knowledge of China at that time was slight and inaccurate. The Spanish Sovereigns, as their letter of introduction furnished to Columbus indicates, thought that the Mongol dynasty of Kubla Khan still reigned in the Celestial Empire, although the Ming dynasty had supplanted it as far back as 1368. Most of the information (and misinformation) that Europe had about China came from *The Book of Ser Marco Polo*, the Venetian who spent about three years in China around the turn of the fourteenth century. This account of his experiences was circulated in countless manuscript copies and was one of the earliest books to be printed. Marco Polo not only confirmed the rumors that Chinese emperors were rolling in wealth, but he wrote a highly embellished account of an even wealthier island kingdom named Cipangu (Japan) which, he said, lay 1500 miles off the coast of China.

We must constantly keep in mind that nobody in Europe had any conception or suspicion of the existence of the continent that we call America. The voyages of the Northmen in the eleventh century to a part of the east coast of the future Canada or New England, which they called Vinland, were either unknown or forgotten in Southern Europe; and if Columbus had heard about them on his voyage to Iceland, they were of no interest to him, since he was not interested in wild grapes, pine trees and codfish, but in gold and spices. Everyone regarded the Ocean Sea as one and indivisible, flowing around Europe, Asia and Africa, which formed, as it were, one big island in one big ocean. The great questions before Columbus, and before the various monarchs and officials who must decide whether or not to support him, were, "How far west *is* the Far East? How many miles lie between Spain and China or Japan? How long would the voyage take? And is such a voyage practicable?"

Everyone, we repeat, admitted that the Earth was a sphere, and the convention of dividing a circle or sphere into 360 degrees had been arrived at by the Greeks. But how long was a degree? On your answer to that depended your estimate of the size of the Earth. Ptolemy of Alexandria, whose book was the geographical Bible of Columbus's day, said that it was 50 nautical miles [1] long — the correct measure is 60. Alfragan, a Moslem geographer of the ninth century, said the degree measured 66 nautical miles, but Columbus misread him and decided that Alfragan's degree was 45 miles long and that Alfragan, not Ptolemy, was right. In other words, he underestimated the size of the world by 25 per cent.

Besides this mistake on the size of the globe, Columbus made another colossal error in reckoning how far eastward Asia stretched. The actual combined length of Europe and Asia is roughly 130 degrees from Cape St. Vincent to Peiping, or 150 degrees to Tokyo. Ptolemy guessed that it was 180 degrees, which was half the circumference of the globe. Marinus of Tyre, an earlier authority whom Columbus naturally preferred, stretched out this land mass to 225 degrees. Marco Polo, who took two or three years to cross Asia by land, made some rough calculations and tacked on 28 degrees more for China and 30 degrees additional for Japan; this, added to Marinus's 225 degrees, would place Tokyo on the meridian that runs through Western Cuba, Chattanooga,

---

[1] I use in this book the standard nautical mile of 2000 yards, which is equivalent to one minute of latitude or to one minute of longitude on the equator. The old authorities I quote used different units, but I have reduced them all to nautical miles.

Grand Rapids and Western Ontario! Moreover, as Columbus proposed to jump off from the western Canary Islands, which lie on a parallel 9 degrees west of Cape St. Vincent, he figured he would have only 68 degrees of westing to make before hitting the coast of Japan. Combining that gross miscalculation with his underestimate of the length of a degree, he figured that the length of the ocean voyage from the Canaries to Japan would be 2400 nautical miles. The actual air-line distance is 10,600 miles!

Columbus did not, however, come to this conclusion all by himself. He had the support of a learned physician of Florence, Paolo Toscanelli, who dabbled in astronomy and mathematics. Toscanelli, believing Marco Polo's estimate of the length of Asia to be correct, had written to a Portuguese friend in 1474, urging him to persuade the King to organize a voyage west to Japan, "most fertile in gold," and to the Chinese province of Mangi. He envisioned a voyage of 3000 miles from Lisbon to Cipangu (Japan) and 5000 miles from Lisbon to Quinsay (Hangchow), and sent a chart to demonstrate his theory. Columbus, tremendously excited when he heard about this, wrote to the Florentine sage asking for more details, and received an encouraging letter and another chart, which he carried with him on his great voyage of discovery. This correspondence took place shortly after Columbus's return from the Gold Coast, in 1481 or early 1482. The Toscanelli letter and chart were always his Exhibits "A" and "B."

Of course he had other exhibits as well: some literary, others practical. There were plenty of Biblical texts besides Psalm 19 — "The isles that are in the sea shall be troubled at thy departure" (Ezekiel xxvi 18), "And His dominion shall be from sea even to sea, and from the river even to the ends of the earth" (Zechariah ix 10; repeated in Psalm 72, verse 8), "The isles saw it, and feared; the ends of the earth were afraid, drew near, and came" (Isaiah xli 5). Aristotle was said to have written that one could cross the

Ocean from Spain to the Indies in a few days. Strabo, the Greek geographer who lived at the time of Christ, wrote that it had actually been attempted by mariners of his day, who returned "through want of resolution and the scarcity of provisions." Pierre d'Ailly's *Imago Mundi*, Columbus's bedside book for years — his copy, still preserved at Seville, is covered by hundreds of manuscript notes — insisted that the Ocean was "of no great width" between Morocco and the eastern coast of Asia, that it could be navigated in a few days with a fair wind.

Thus, very early in the game, Columbus, absolutely convinced of the truth of his theory, brushed aside all doubts and difficulties and began collecting every possible text or quotation that could be used to support it. For instance, the statement in the apocryphal Second Book of Esdras (vi 42), "Six parts hast thou dried up," was frequently used by Columbus to prove that six sevenths of the globe is land; *ergo,* the Ocean covers only one seventh of the globe and cannot be very broad.

On the practical side, in the course of his voyages he observed evidence such as exotic tree trunks and "horse-beans," which are the fruit of an American mimosa, washed ashore in the Azores; the flat-faced corpses seen at Galway, who, if Chinese, could not have floated many thousand miles without decomposing; numerous reports of islands west of the Azores and the Canaries. For Columbus did not assume that he had to make his transoceanic voyage in one jump. There was no reason to suppose that Flores and Corvo were the last islands before you hit "The Indies." The legendary voyages of Saint Brendan, the Irish seagoing monk of the sixth century, were believed to be true, and the Portuguese had their own legend about the Island of Antilia, settled by refugees from the Moorish wars in the eighth century. An old salt in Lisbon even claimed he had been there and had been chased out. Toscanelli, too, mentioned Antilia as a convenient island of call, and, as we shall see, Columbus made a brief search for it on his First Voyage.

In 1484 he made his first effort to interest a prince — John II, King of Portugal, a nephew of Henry the Navigator who was intensely interested in new discoveries. According to the contemporary Portuguese historians and chroniclers, the Columbian project was exactly the same then as later — to reach Japan by sailing west and to discover other islands en route. "The King," says one of the historians, "as he observed this *Christovão Colom* to be a big talker and boastful . . . and full of fancy and imagination with his Isle *Cypango* . . . gave him small credit." Nevertheless, the King committed the project to a junta consisting of a prominent churchman and two Jewish physicians of reputed skill in celestial navigation. They turned it down, flat. Their reasons for so doing are not recorded, but we may assume that they had a more accurate idea of the distance to be covered than did Columbus.

It may be, however, that Columbus simply asked too much, since the kings of Portugal were accustomed to having their discoveries made free. There are about a dozen records of the monarch granting one of his captains an island, such as one of the Azores, or an island west of the Azores, if he could find it. In the very year 1485, when the King's committee rejected Columbus's project, he gave permission to two Portuguese mariners, Dulmo and Estreito, to set forth and discover Antilia at their own proper charge and expense. If they found it, they would be hereditary captains there and receive suitable honors and titles. They agreed to sail west for forty days and then return if they found nothing.

It is obvious why this and all other pre-Columbian Portuguese attempts to discover islands west of the Azores failed. In the first place, there was no Antilia, and no island nearer than Newfoundland; in the second place, to sail west from the Azores, as all these men did, one had to buck westerly winds in high latitudes. Columbus, in his African voyages, had observed the steady easterly tradewinds between the Equator and the latitude of the Canaries, and so chose the Canaries as his point of departure. That is the plain reason why he succeeded in finding something, even though it was not what he wanted.

Before Christopher could try it his way, he must have money and support. In 1485, the same year that the Portuguese committee turned him down, his wife Dona Felipa died at Lisbon. That broke his strongest tie with Portugal. Nobody there would stake him if the King would not, so Columbus decided to try his luck in Spain. He knew no one there except a sister of his late wife who was married to a Spaniard in Huelva, so to that part of Spain, the County of Niebla adjoining Portugal, Columbus took ship with his five-year-old son Diego.

It must have been with sinking heart that Columbus entered the Rio Saltés and sighted the sleepy little ports of Huelva and Palos, a sad contrast to bright, bustling Lisbon. As his ship rounded into the Rio Tinto, he observed on a bluff the buildings of the Franciscan friary of La Rábida. That suggested a solution to his problem of what to do with Diego, as the Franciscans were known to take "boarders." So, after landing at Palos, he walked with his little son four miles to the friary, knocked at the gate and asked the porter for a drink of water and some bread for the boy. Fortunately, Antonio de Marchena, a highly intelligent Franciscan who had studied astronomy, came to the gate and got into conversation with Columbus. He invited both father and son to stay, accepted Diego as a pupil and introduced Columbus to the Count of Medina Celi, a grandee of Spain and also an important shipowner of Cadiz.

Medina Celi, of whom Columbus asked "three or four well-equipped caravels, and no more," had almost decided to underwrite the enterprise when it occurred to him to ask permission of the Queen. He did so, and Isabella refused, believing that so important an enterprise as that of Columbus should be conducted by the crown. But this transfer from Count to Queen postponed Columbus's voyage some six years.

CHAPTER IV

Bargaining with Princes

ABOUT NINE MONTHS elapsed before Columbus could obtain an audience with the Queen, because the court was traveling from city to city in central and northern Spain, and he had no funds to follow. From Seville, where his negotiations with Medina Celi had taken place, he went to the nearby city of Cordova to await the Queen's good pleasure.

At Cordova, as in most cities of the Peninsula, there was already a colony of Genoese, one of whom was an apothecary; and apothecary shops in those days were meeting places for physicians and amateur scientists. Columbus naturally dropped in at the shop of his compatriot, and here became acquainted with a frequenter of the informal club, Diego de Harana. Diego invited him to his house, where he met a twenty-year-old country cousin of the Haranas, Beatriz Enríquez. She became Columbus's mistress and in 1488 bore him his second son, Ferdinand. The fact that Columbus never married Beatriz has troubled his more pious biographers, as, judging from certain provisions for her in his will, it troubled his conscience; but nobody at the time seems to have held this lapse of morals against him. His wife had been a lady of rank who helped him to establish a position in Portugal, and according to the standards of the day, a second marriage with a peasant's daughter would have been unsuitable for one who intended to be a nobleman and admiral. The Harana family were pleased with the connection; at least two Haranas subsequently served under Columbus, and the friendship between them and the legitimate Colóns continued for two or three generations.

On May Day 1486, almost a year from the time he had first set foot in Spain, Columbus was received by the Queen in the Alcazar that still stands at Cordova. Isabella the Catholic was one of the ablest European sovereigns in an age of strong kings. She had an intuitive faculty for choosing the right man for a job, and for doing the right thing at the right time. She was very close to Columbus's age and similar to him in temperament, and in coloring – blue eyes and auburn hair. Her marriage with Ferdinand of Aragon had united all "the Spains," excepting Portugal, to which she was allied, and the remnant of the Moorish Caliphate of Cordova, which she had resolved to conquer. Some spark of understanding evidently passed between Christopher and Isabella at their first meeting, and although she turned down his enterprise more than once, he found that he could count on her in the end. On this occasion she appointed a special commission under Hernando de Talavera, her confessor, to examine the Great Project and recommend whether she should accept or reject it, or allow Medina Celi to back it.

Then began a period of almost six years, the most unhappy in Columbus's entire life. He had to sustain a continual battle against prejudice, contumely and sheer indifference. A proud, sensitive man who *knew* that his project was feasible and that it would open new pathways to maritime achievement and opportunity, he had to endure clownish witticisms and crackpot jests by ignorant courtiers, to be treated worse than a beggar, and at times actually to suffer want. Worst of all, perhaps, he learned by experience the meaning of the phrase *cosas de España*, the irritating procrastination of Spaniards, who never seemed to be able to make up their minds, to carry out a plain order, or to make a firm decision without fees or favors. In later years he often alluded bitterly to these experiences and tactlessly contrasted the enormous wealth and power he had conferred on Spain with his pitiable and protracted efforts to obtain a fair hearing.

The Talavera commission, meeting at Salamanca [1] around Christmastide 1486, could not reach an agreement. At least one member, Diego de Deza, was in favor of the Great Enterprise, and it was doubtless due to his influence, or Talavera's, that early in 1487 Columbus was given a retaining fee of 12,000 maravedis a year. [2] That was the pay of an able seaman, enough to support a man of Columbus's simple tastes, if it had been paid regularly.

Month followed month, another Christmas passed, but nothing issued from the Talavera commission. So, early in 1488, Columbus wrote to John II of Portugal, requesting another hearing and asking for a safe-conduct from arrest for his unpaid bills in Lisbon. The King replied promptly and most cordially, urging Columbus to come immediately, and promising protection from lawsuit or arrest. There were probably two reasons for this sudden and flattering change of attitude — Dulmo and Estreito had not located the mythical Island of Antilia, and Bartholomew Dias, embarked on perhaps the twentieth Portuguese attempt to reach the Indies by rounding Africa, had been gone seven months and nothing had been heard from him.

For want of funds, Christopher was delayed in leaving for Lisbon, and before he and his brother Bartholomew (who had remained there) could "do business" with John II, Dias returned.

---

[1] It is this commission whose deliberations have been so distorted by Washington Irving and others as a debate on whether the world was a sphere or not. Actually, we know nothing definite about the arguments, but we may be certain that since the commission consisted of men of learning, the sphericity of the earth never came into question.

[2] To convey the equivalent of Spanish currency of this era, I have tried to state the gold content in British and U. S. coinage before both countries went off the gold standard. Thus, 12,000 maravedis equalled $83 in gold (four double eagles plus $3.00), or 16½ guineas.

The Columbus brothers were present in December 1488 when the three caravels commanded by Dias sailed proudly up the Tagus. Their great captain had rounded the south cape of Africa — the Cape of Good Hope the King named it — and was well on his way up the east coast when his men mutinied and forced him to turn back. That ended King John's interest in Columbus. His man had found a sea route to the Indies, so why invest money in the doubtful West-to-the-Orient project?

Moreover, Columbus had a rival in Portugal, Martin Behaim, a young Nuremberger who like him had made voyages under the Portuguese flag and married the daughter of a Portuguese master mariner. Behaim's ideas of the size of the Earth and the length of Asia, incorporated in a globe that he constructed in 1492, were almost identical with those of Columbus, and in 1493, just too late, he proposed to John II to do exactly what Columbus had done, or thought he had done.

Around New Year's, 1489, the Columbus brothers decided on a plan of action. Christopher returned to Spain, where he still had hopes from the slow-moving Talavera commission, while Bartholomew wound up the chart-making business and embarked on a long journey to try to sell the West-to-the-Orient project to some other prince. Unable to make any impression on Henry VII of England, Bartholomew proceeded to France, where Anne de Beaujeu, sister to King Charles VIII, befriended him and employed him to make charts for her at Fontainebleau. Through her, Bartholomew became friendly with the French King but never obtained any certain prospect of his support.

Success to Christopher always seemed to be just around the corner, but in 1489 he still had three years to wait before obtaining anything definite. We know very little of how he passed the time. According to one contemporary, he started a branch of "Columbus Brothers, Chartmakers and Booksellers" at Seville. The Queen took notice of his return to Castile by giving him an open letter to all local officials, ordering them to furnish him board and lodging en route to court, which was then in a fortified camp outside the Moorish city of Baza, under siege by the Spanish army. There is some indication that Christopher joined the army as a volunteer while waiting for an answer, and he certainly had the time to fire a few shots at the infidels.

Not until late in 1490 did the Talavera commission issue its report, and it was unfavorable. The experts advised the Queen that the West-to-the-Orient project "rested on weak foundations"; that its attainment seemed "uncertain and impossible to any educated person"; that the proposed voyage to Asia would require three years' time, even if the ships could return, which they judged doubtful; that the Ocean was infinitely larger than Columbus supposed, and much of it unnavigable. And finally, it was not likely that God would have allowed any uninhabited lands of real value to be concealed from His people for so many centuries. Rejection could not have been more flat, and we must admit that all the commission's arguments, save the last, were sound. Suppose there had been no America, no ship then built, however resolute her master and crew, or frugal in provision, could have made the ten-thousand-mile voyage from Spain to Japan.

Apparently a complete deadlock. Columbus knew he could do it; the experts were certain he could not. It needed something as powerful as feminine intuition to break the log jam.

For the present, all the Queen would do was to give Columbus fresh hope. He could apply again, said she, when the war with the Moors was over. He waited almost another year and then decided to leave Spain and join his brother in France. Calling at the La Rábida friary near Palos to pick up his son Diego, now about ten years old, he was persuaded by the prior, Father Juan Pérez, to give the Queen another chance, and wrote to her to that

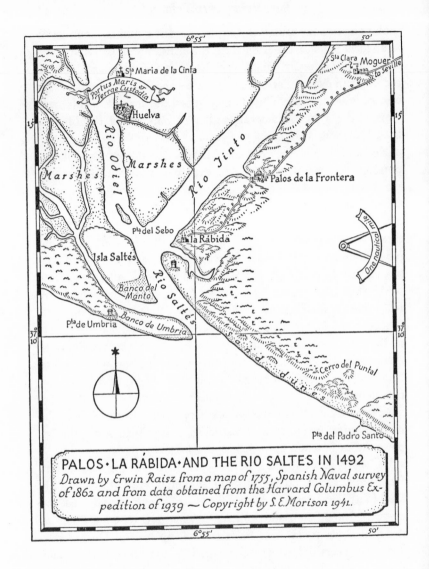

PALOS · LA RÁBIDA · AND THE RIO SALTES IN 1492
Drawn by Erwin Raisz from a map of 1755, Spanish Naval survey of 1862 and from data obtained from the Harvard Columbus Expedition of 1939 — Copyright by S.E.Morison 1941.

effect. She replied by summoning Columbus to court, and sent him a generous gift to buy himself some decent clothing and a mule.

Columbus always found more friends and supporters among priests than among laymen. They seemed to understand him better, since his thoughts and aspirations were permeated with religious emotion. He was far more particular than most laymen in saying the daily offices of the church — prime, tierce, sext, none and compline. He seldom missed an opportunity to attend Mass, and in an age of picturesque and elaborate profanity, he was never heard to utter any other oath than "By San Fernando!" or to curse, except that he would blurt out, "May God take you!" when exasperated. He had a fine presence and an innate dignity that impressed people, of whatever estate, and although he never spoke perfect hidalgo Castilian, it was not expected that he should, as Genoa-born and of long residence in Portugal.

At about Christmas time 1491, Columbus again appeared at court, which was then being held in the fortified camp of Santa Fe during the siege of Granada. A new commission was appointed, and the Royal Council reviewed their findings. The exact details are not known, but it seems probable that the commission, reading the Queen's mind, recommended that Columbus be allowed to try this project, and that the Council rejected it because of the price he asked. For this extraordinary man, despite poverty, delays and discouragement, had actually raised his demands. In 1485 he had been willing to sail west for Medina Celi on an expense-account basis, without any particular honors or emoluments. Now he demanded not only ennoblement and the title of Admiral, but also that he be made governor and viceroy of any new lands he might discover, that both titles be hereditary in his family, and that he and his heirs be given a ten per cent cut on the trade. He had suffered so many outrages and insults during his long residence in Spain that — by San Fernando! — he would not glorify Spain for nothing. If the Sovereigns would grant him, contingent on his success, such rank, titles and property that he and his issue could hold up their heads with Spanish grandees, well and good; but no more bargaining. Take it, Your Majesties, or leave it.

Leave it they did, in January 1492, immediately after the fall of Granada. Ferdinand and Isabella told him this at an audience that the King, at least, intended to be final. Columbus saddled his mule, packed the saddlebags with his charts and other exhibits, and started for Seville with his faithful friend Juan Pérez, intending to take ship for France and join Bartholomew in a fresh appeal to Charles VIII.

Just as, in Oriental bargaining, a storekeeper will often run after a departing customer to accept his last offer, so it happened here. Luis de Santangel, keeper of King Ferdinand's privy purse, called on the Queen the very day that Columbus left Santa Fe and urged her to meet Columbus's terms. The expedition, he pointed out, would not cost as much as a week's entertainment of a fellow sovereign, and he would undertake to raise the money himself. As for the honors and emoluments, Columbus asked only for a promise of them in the event of his success, and if he did succeed, they would be a small price to pay for the discovery of new islands and a western route to the Indies. Isabella, who had probably felt that way all along, jumped at this, her really last chance. She even proposed to pledge her crown jewels for the expenses, but Santangel said that would not be necessary. And she sent a messenger who overtook Columbus at a village four miles from Santa Fe, and brought him back.

Although everything was now decided in principle, there were plenty more *cosas de España* to be overcome, and it was not until April 1492 that the contracts between Columbus and the Sovereigns, the Capitulations, as they are generally called, were signed and sealed. Therein the Sovereigns, in consideration that Cristóbal Colón (as henceforth Columbus called himself) is setting forth "to discover and acquire certain islands and mainlands in the Ocean Sea," promise him to be Admiral of the Ocean Sea,[3] Viceroy and Governor of lands that he may discover. He shall have ten per cent of all gold, gems, spices or other merchandise produced or obtained by trade within those domains, tax free; he shall have the right to invest in one eighth of any ship going thither; and these offices and emoluments will be enjoyed by his heirs and successors forever. The sovereigns also issued to him a brief passport in Latin, stating that they were sending him with three caravels "toward the regions of India" (*ad partes Indie*), and three identical letters of introduction, one to the "Grand Khan" (the Chinese Emperor) and the other two with a blank space so that the proper titles of other princes could be inserted.

It will doubtless seem impossibly naïve to the modern reader that anyone could expect Columbus to land somewhere on the coast of China or Japan with less than one hundred men, and "take over." But Europe was then very ignorant of the Far East; the Portuguese had had no difficulty in dealing with Negro kings in Africa, so why shouldn't Columbus do the same thing in Asia? Moreover, the colony that Columbus had in mind was not what we mean by a colony, but a trading factory. The trading factory (what we would call a trading post) had long been familiar to Europeans. It was an extension of one country's sovereignty into another's, for commercial purposes; it might be armed, if in a relatively savage region, like the Genoese trading factory in the Crimea or the Portuguese São Jorge da Mina on the Gold Coast; or it might be a peaceful extra-territorial settlement, such as the

[3] Columbus's title of Admiral had nothing to do with command of a fleet; it meant that he would have admiralty jurisdiction over the Ocean and any new lands discovered. His title when commanding a fleet on any of his four voyages was Captain General, corresponding to our Commodore.

Hanseatic League's Steelyard in London, and the Merchants Adventurers' factory in Amsterdam. The 1492 globe of Martin Behaim, who shared Columbus's geographical ideas, shows an archipelago south of Japan, corresponding to the Ryukyus; if there had been no American barrier, and the Ocean had been as narrow as Columbus supposed, he doubtless would have established a trading factory on an island like Okinawa, which would have become an important entrepôt between China and the West, both for commerce and missionary effort. That was no extravagant expectation, as is proved by the fact that, eighty years later in the Philippines, Legaspi occupied the site of Manila for Spain and built the old city with no more force than Columbus had, and no prince or potentate objected. Manila became an immensely valuable trading factory where the products of Spain were exchanged for those of China.

It may also seem odd that the Sovereigns should have consented to give Columbus so much as ten per cent of expected profits. It was, however, then usual throughout Europe for princes to reward their servants and subjects in that manner, and it is still done in Eastern countries: Abdulla Dawaish, Prime Minister of the Arabian Sultanate of El Katar or Quttar on the Persian Gulf, gets ten per cent of all imports and exports, including oil, in 1954. There was good reason for this sort of financial expedient in the fifteenth century, when the revenues of princes were relatively low, and the resistance of their subjects to taxation had not been broken down by habit and necessity.

CHAPTER V

Preparations for the First Voyage

ALTHOUGH it was now settled in principle, the success of the Enterprise depended on an infinite number of practical details. First, it was decided to fit out the fleet and recruit the men at Palos, the little port in the Niebla where Columbus had first set foot in Spain, and for several reasons. Columbus had made friends there of the Pinzón family, leading shipowners and master mariners; both ships and sailors were available. And Palos had committed some municipal misdemeanor for which the Queen conveniently fined her two well-equipped caravels. Columbus made a public appearance in the Church of St. George, Palos, on May 23, 1492, with his friend Fray Juan Pérez, while a notary read the royal order that "within ten days" the two caravels were to be provided and crews recruited, with four months' advance pay.

Ten days, of course, was preposterous, and it actually took about three months for Columbus to get to sea. He had been promised three caravels, not two, but it so happened that a ship from Galicia, owned and captained by Juan de la Cosa, was then in port, and Columbus chartered her as his flagship.

Santa María, as this ship was called, is the most famous of Columbus's ships. She left her bones on a reef off Hispaniola, and no picture or model of her has survived, but several conjectural models have been made and two full-size "replicas" have been constructed in Spain. The original *Santa María* was probably of about 100 tons' burthen, which meant that her cargo capacity was

100 "tuns" or double hogsheads of wine. Her rig was the conventional one of the period, when ships were just emerging from the one-big-mast type of the Middle Ages: a mainmast higher than she was long, a main yard as long as the keel, carrying an immense square sail — the main course — which was counted on to do most of the driving. Above the main course was spread a small main topsail. The foremast, little more than half the height of the mainmast, carried only a square fore course or foresail. The mizzenmast, stepped on the high poop, carried a small lateen-rigged sail, and under the bowsprit, which pointed up from the bows at a sharp angle, was spread a small square sail called the spritsail, which performed rather inefficiently the function of the modern jib.

A Spanish ship in those days had an official name, usually that of a saint, and a nickname which the sailors used; *Santa María* was *La Gallega*, "The Galician." One of the two caravels provided by the town of Palos was named *Santa Clara*, but she is universally known by her nickname *Niña*, so given because she belonged to the Niño family of Palos. *Niña* was Columbus's favorite. She carried him safely home from his First Voyage, took him to western Cuba and back to Spain on the Second, and made another voyage to Hispaniola. She measured about 60 tons, her length was not over 70 feet, and at the start she was rigged with three lateen sails, like a Portuguese caravel, but in the Canaries Columbus had her re-rigged square like *Santa María*, because square sails are much handier than lateen rig when running before the wind.

Pinta, also a locally built caravel, was probably a little larger than *Niña*, and square-rigged from the first. Her real name we do not know; *Pinta* probably was derived from a former owner named Pinto. She was a smart sailer; the New World was first sighted from her deck and she was first home to Spain.

All vessels carried inside stone ballast. They were fastened mostly with wooden trunnels or pins, such as one sees in the frames of old American houses; their sides were painted gay colors above the waterline and, below it, payed with pitch, which was supposed to discourage barnacles and teredos. Crosses and heraldic devices were emblazoned on the sails, and the ships carried a variety of large, brightly colored flags which were flown on entering and leaving port. Queen Isabella's royal ensign, quartering the castles and lions of Castile and Leon, was hoisted on the main truck, and on the foremast or mizzen was displayed the special banner of the expedition: a green cross on a white field, with a crown on each arm — a concession to Aragon. All three vessels carried a little crude artillery, to repel possible pirates or other unwelcome boarders, but they were in no sense combatant ships, and carried neither soldiers nor gunners.

Columbus, a foreigner in the Niebla, could never have recruited officers and men without the enthusiastic support of three leading shipping families of Palos — the Pinzóns, Niños and Quinteros. Martín Alonso Pinzón commanded *Pinta* and took his younger brother Francisco along as master, a rank that corresponds roughly to the modern "exec.," or first officer. Another brother, Vicente Yáñez Pinzón, commanded *Niña*, whose master-owner was Juan Niño, and a brother of Juan, Peralonso Niño, piloted *Santa María*. Columbus himself commanded the flagship, but her owner, Juan de la Cosa, remained on board as master. Each vessel had a pilot, an officer who shared the duties of the modern first officer and had charge of navigation, and a surgeon. In the fleet were several specialists — Luis de Torres, a converted Jew who knew Arabic, which, it was thought, would enable him to converse with the Chinese and Japanese; Rodrigo de Escobedo, secretary of the fleet, who would make an official record of discoveries; Rodrigo Sánchez, the royal comptroller, whose main duty was to see that the crown got its share of the gold; and Pedro Gutiérrez, butler of the King's dais, who apparently was tired of court life, since he shipped as chief steward; Diego de Harana, cousin of Columbus's mistress, the marshal of the fleet, corresponding to the old naval rating of master-at-arms. The names of 39 officers and men of *Santa María*, 26 of *Pinta* and 22 of *Niña* are known, and there were probably two or three more, which would bring the total complement of the fleet up to 90.

Almost all the enlisted men — stewards, boatswains, caulkers, able seamen and "gromets," or ship's boys — were from the Niebla or nearby towns of Andalusia like Seville, Cordova and Jerez de la Frontera. Each seaman received about the equivalent of $7 in gold per month, the petty officers twice that and the boys about $4.60. The only foreigners, besides Columbus, were another Genoese, one Portuguese and a Venetian. The story that Columbus had an Englishman and an Irishman on board is a myth, but there is some foundation for the tradition that the crews included jailbirds. Three lads who had been given life imprisonment for helping a condemned murderer to break jail were set free in order to ship with Columbus; they turned out to be trustworthy men and went with the Admiral on later voyages, as did a large number of the others. On the whole, the crews of these ships were good, capable fellows from the neighborhood, with members of three leading families in key positions. Encouraged by an ancient pilot who was sure he had just missed the Indies on a Portuguese voyage westward forty years earlier, these men and boys overcame the natural conservatism of a mariner in the hope of glory, gold and adventure. Those who survived won plenty of the first two, and all shared in one of the greatest adventures of history — Columbus's First Voyage.

CHAPTER VI

First Crossing of the Atlantic

B Y THE SECOND DAY of August, 1492, everything at last was ready. That night every man and boy of the fleet confessed his sins, received absolution and made his communion at the church of Palos, which by happy coincidence was dedicated to Saint George, patron saint of Genoa. Columbus went on board his flagship in the small hours of Friday the third and gave the signal to get under way. Before the sun rose, all three vessels had anchors aweigh, and with sails hanging limp from their yards were floating down the Rio Tinto on the morning ebb, using their long sweeps to maintain steerageway. As they swung into the Saltés and passed La Rábida close aboard, they could hear the friars chanting the ancient hymn *Iam lucis orto sidere* with its haunting refrain *Et nunc et in perpetuum,* which we render "Evermore and evermore."

This fleet of good hope, whose achievements would radically alter world history, sailed parallel to another fleet of misery and woe. On the very same tide there dropped down the Saltés the last vessel carrying the Jews whom Ferdinand and Isabella had expelled from Spain. August 2 was their deadline; any who remained thereafter were to be executed unless they embraced Christianity. Thousands of pitiful refugees, carrying what few household goods they could stow in the crowded ships, were bound for the more tolerant lands of Islam, or for the only Christian country, the Netherlands, which would receive them. Columbus in all his writings dropped no word of pity for the fate of this persecuted race, and even expressed the wish to exclude them from the lands he discovered. But if there had been a new prophet among the Spanish Jews, he might have pointed out the Columbian fleet to his wretched compatriots on that August morning and said, "Behold the ships that in due time will carry the children of Israel to the ends of the earth."

Columbus's plan for the voyage was simple, and its simplicity insured his success. Not for him the boisterous head winds, the monstrous seas and the dark, unbridled waters of the North Atlantic, which had already baffled so many Portuguese. He would run south before the prevailing northerlies to the Canary Islands, and there make, as it were, a right-angle turn; for he had observed on his African voyages that the winter winds in the latitude of the Canaries blew from the east, and that the ocean around them, more often than not, was calm as a millpond. An even better reason to take his departure from the Canaries was their position astride latitude 28 degrees North, which, he believed, cut Japan, passing en route the mythical Isle of Antilia, which would make a good break in the westward passage. Until about a hundred years ago when chronometers became generally available to find longitude, sailors always tried to find the latitude of their destination and then would "run their westing" (or easting) down until they hit it.[1] That is what Columbus proposed to do with respect to Japan, which he had figured out to be only 2400 nautical miles due west of the Canaries.

The first leg of the voyage was made in less than a week. Then, within sight of the Grand Canary, the fleet ran into a calm that lasted two or three days. Columbus decided to send *Pinta* into Las Palmas for some needed repairs while *Santa María* and *Niña*

---

[1] A New England shipmaster of whom someone inquired the route from Cape Cod to Barbados said, "Run South until your butter melts, then West!"

went to Gomera, westernmost of the Canaries that the Spaniards had wrested from their native inhabitants. At Gomera the Captain General (as we should call Columbus on this voyage before he made Admiral) sent men ashore to fill extra water casks, buy breadstuffs and cheese, and put a supply of native beef in pickle. He then sailed to Las Palmas to superintend *Pinta's* repairs and returned with her to Gomera.

On September 2 all three ships were anchored off San Sebastián, the port of that island. Columbus then met for the first time Doña Beatriz de Bobadilla, widow of the former captain of the island. Beatriz was a beautiful lady still under thirty, and Columbus is said to have fallen in love with her; but if that is true, he did not love her warmly enough to tarry to the next full moon. Additional ship's stores were quickly hoisted on board and struck below, and on September 6, 1492, the fleet weighed anchor for the last time in the Old World. They had still another island to pass, the lofty Ferro or Hierro. Owing to calms and variables Ferro and the 12,000-foot peak of Tenerife were in sight until the ninth, but by nightfall that day, every trace of land had sunk below the eastern horizon, and the three vessels were alone on an uncharted ocean. Columbus himself gave out the course: "West; nothing to the north, nothing to the south."

Before going into the details of the voyage, let us see how those vessels were navigated, and how a day was passed at sea. Celestial navigation was then in its infancy, but rough estimates of latitude could be made from the height of the North Star above the horizon and its relation to the two outer stars (the "Guards") of the Little Dipper. A meridian altitude of the sun, applied to available tables of the sun's declination, also gave latitude, by a simple formula. But the instruments of observation — a solid wood or brass quadrant and the seaman's astrolabe — were so crude, and the movement of a ship threw them off to such an extent, that most navigators took their latitude sights ashore. Columbus relied almost completely on "dead reckoning," which means plotting your course and position on a chart from the three elements of direction, time and distance.

The direction he had from one or more compasses which were similar to those used in small craft until recently — a circular card graduated to the 32 points (N, N by E, NNE, NE by N, NE, and so on), with a lodestone under the north point, mounted on a pin and enclosed in a binnacle with gimbals so it could swing freely with the motion of the ship. Columbus's standard compass was mounted on the poop deck where the officer of the watch could see it. The helmsman, who steered with a heavy tiller attached directly to the rudder head, was below decks and could see very little. He may have had another compass to steer by, but in the smaller vessels, at least, he was conned by the officer of the deck and kept a steady course by the feel of the helm. On a sailing vessel you can do that; it would be impossible in any power craft.

Time on the vessels of that day was measured by a half-hour glass which hung from a beam so the sand could flow freely from the upper to the lower half. As soon as the sand was all down, a ship's boy turned the glass and the officer of the deck recorded it by making a stroke on a slate. Eight glasses made a watch; the modern ship's bells were originally a means of marking the glasses. This half-hour-glass time could be corrected daily in fair weather by noting the moment when the sun lay due south, which was local noon.

Distance was the most variable of these three elements. Columbus had no chip log or other method of measuring the speed of his vessels. He and the watch officers merely estimated it and noted it down. By carefully checking Columbus's Journal of his First Voyage, Captain J. W. McElroy ascertained that he made an average 9 per cent overestimate of his distance. This did not prevent his finding the way home, because the mistake was constant, and time and course were correct. It only resulted in Columbus placing the islands of his discovery farther west than they really were.

Even after making the proper reduction for this overestimate, the speed of his vessels is surprising. Ships of that day were expected to make 3 to 5 knots in a light breeze, up to 9½ in a strong, fair gale, and at times to be capable of 12 knots. In October 1492, on the outward passage, the Columbus fleet made an average of 142 miles per day for five consecutive days, and the best day's run, 182 miles, averaged 8 knots. On the homeward passage, in February 1493, *Niña* and *Pinta* covered 198 miles one day, and at times hit it up to 11 knots. Any yachtsman today would be proud to make the records that the great Admiral did on some of his transatlantic crossings in the fifteenth century. Improvements in sailing vessels since 1492 have been more in seaworthiness and comfort than in speed.

One reason Columbus always wanted two or more vessels was to have someone to rescue survivors in case of sinking. But he made an unusual record for that era by never losing a ship at sea, unless we count the *Santa María*, grounded without loss of life. Comforts and conveniences were almost totally lacking. Cooking was done on deck over a bed of sand in a wooden firebox protected from the wind by a hood. The diet was a monotonous one of salt meat, hardtack and dried peas. For drink they had wine, while it lasted, and water in casks, which often went bad. Only the Captain General and the ships' captains had cabins with bunks; the others slept where they could, in their clothes.

In those days, sailors were the most religious of laymen. On each vessel a boy was charged with singing a ditty at daybreak, which began:

> Blessed be the light of day
> And the Holy Cross, we say;

after which he recited the Lord's Prayer and the Ave Maria, and invoked a blessing on the ship's company. Every half hour a boy sang out when turning the glass. For instance, at what we would call five bells, he sang:

> Five is past and six floweth,
> More shall flow if God willeth,
> Count and pass make voyage fast.

After sunset, and before the first night watch was set, all hands were called to evening prayers. The service began with the boy whose duty it was to light the binnacle lamp singing:

> God give us a good night and good sailing;
> May our ship make a good passage,
> Sir Captain and Master and good company.

All hands then said the Lord's Prayer, the Creed and the Ave Maria, and concluded by singing the *Salve Regina*. Here are the correct words and music of the ancient Benedictine chant, but as Columbus himself said, "Seamen sing or say it after their own fashion," bawling it out in several keys at once and murdering the stately Latin words. But was it the less acceptable to the Virgin, under whose protection all sailors felt secure?

Now the boy who turns up the glass for the eighth time sings:

> The watch is called,
> The glass floweth.
> We shall make a good voyage
> If God willeth.

And as the vessels sail westward through the soft tropic night, rolling and pitching, sails bellying and slatting, cordage straining, bows throwing foam, every half hour is marked by this chantey:

SALVE REGINA

To our God let's pray
To give us a good voyage,
And through the Blessed Mother,
Our advocate on high,
Protect us from the waterspout
And send no tempest nigh.

So much for the sea ritual that went on every day, whatever the weather. Now for the events of the voyage.

On September 9, the day he dropped the last land below the horizon, Columbus decided to keep a true reckoning of his course for his own use and a false one to give out to the people, so that they would not be frightened at sailing so far from land. But, owing to his overestimate of speed, the "false" reckoning was more nearly correct than the "true"!

During the first ten days (September 9 to 18), the easterly trade wind blew steadily, and the fleet made 1163 nautical miles' westing. This was the honeymoon of the voyage. *Que era plazer grande el gusto de las mañanas* — "What a delight was the savor of the mornings!" wrote Columbus in his Journal. That entry speaks to the heart of anyone who has sailed in the trades; it recalls the beauty of the dawn, kindling clouds and sails rose color, the smell of dew drying on a wooden deck, and, something Columbus didn't have, the first cup of coffee. Since his ships were at the northern edge of the northeast trades, where the wind first strikes the water, the sea was smooth, and the air, remarked the Captain General in his Journal, was "like April in Andalusia; the only thing wanting was to hear the song of the nightingale." But there were plenty of other birds following the ships: the little Mother Carey's chickens, dabbling for plankton in the bow waves and wakes; the boatswain bird, so called (as old seamen used to say) because it carries a marlinspike in its tail; the man-of-war or frigate bird, "thou ship of the air that never furl'st thy sails," as

Walt Whitman wrote; and when the fleet passed beyond the range of these birds, the big Jaeger gulls gave it a call. During this period the fleet encountered its first field of sargassum or gulfweed and found that it was no hindrance to navigation. "Saw plenty weed" was an almost daily notation in the Captain General's log. The gulfweed bothered him much less than observing a westerly variation of the compass, for in European waters the variation is always easterly.

On September 19, only ten days out from Ferro, the fleet temporarily ran into an area of variable winds and rain. It was near the point on Columbus's chart where the fabled island of Antilia should have been, and all hands expected to sight land. The Captain General even had the deep-sea lead hove, and found no bottom at 200 fathoms; no wonder, since the ocean is about 2300 fathoms deep at the point he had reached. But the seamen who, on the tenth day of the northeast trades, were beginning to wonder whether they could ever beat back home were cheered by the change of wind.

During the next five days only 234 miles were made good. During this spell of moderate weather it was easy to converse from ship to ship and to talk about this or that island, St. Brendan's or Antilia, which they might pick up. In the middle of one of these colloquies, a seamen of *Pinta* gave the "Land Ho!" and everyone thought he saw an island against the setting sun. Columbus fell on his knees to thank God, ordered *Gloria in excelsis Deo* to be sung by all hands, and set a course for the island. But at dawn no island was visible; there was none. It was simply a cloud bank above the western horizon resembling land, a common phenomenon at sea. Martín Alonso Pinzón apparently wished to beat about and search for this island, but Columbus refused, because, he said, "his object was to reach the Indies, and if he delayed, it would not have made sense."

The trade wind now returned, but moderately, and during the six days September 26 to October 1, the fleet made only 382 miles. Under these circumstances the people began to mutter and grumble. Three weeks was probably more than they had ever been outside sight of land before. They were all getting on each other's nerves, as happens even nowadays on a long voyage to a known destination. There was nothing for the men to do in the light wind except to follow the ship's routine, and troll for fish. Grievances, real or imaginary, were blown up; cliques were formed; Spain was farther away every minute, and what lay ahead? Probably nothing, except in the eye of that cursed Genoese. Let's make him turn back, or throw him overboard!

On the first day of October the wind increased, and in five days (October 2 to 6) the fleet made 710 miles. On the sixth, when they had passed longitude 65 degrees West and actually lay directly north of Puerto Rico, Martín Alonso Pinzón shot his agile *Pinta* under the flagship's stern and shouted, "Alter course, sir, to southwest by west . . . Japan!" Columbus did not understand whether Martín Alonso meant that he thought they had missed Japan and should steer southwest by west for China, or that Japan lay in that direction; but he knew and Pinzón knew that the fleet had sailed more than the 2400 miles which, according to their calculations, lay between the Canaries and Japan. Naturally Columbus was uneasy, but he held to the west course magnetic, which, owing to the variation for which he did not allow, was about west by south, true.

On October 7, when there was another false landfall, great flocks of birds passed over the ships, flying westsouthwest; this was the autumn migration from eastern North America to the West Indies. Columbus decided that he had better follow the birds rather than his chart, and changed course accordingly that evening. That was "good joss"; it was his shortest course to the nearest land. Now, every night, the men were heartened by seeing against the moon (full on October 5) flocks of birds flying their way. But by the tenth, mutiny flared up again. No land for thirty-one days. Even by the phony reckoning which Columbus gave out they had sailed much farther west than anyone had expected. Enough of this nonsense, sailing west to nowhere; let the Captain General turn back or else — ! Columbus, says the record, "cheered them as best he could, holding out good hope of the advantages they might gain; and, he added, it was useless to complain, *since he had come to go to the Indies, and so had to continue until he found them, with Our Lord's help.*"

That was typical of Columbus's determination. Yet even he, conscious of divine guidance, could not have kept on indefinitely without the support of his captains and officers. According to one account, it was Martín Alonso Pinzón who cheered him by shouting, *Adelante! Adelante!* which an American poet has translated, "Sail on! Sail on!" But, according to Oviedo, one of the earliest historians who talked with the participants, it was Columbus alone who persuaded the Pinzóns and La Cosa to sail on, with the promise that if land were not found within three days, he would turn back. If this version is correct, as I believe it is, the Captain General's promise to his captains was made on October 9. Next day the trade wind blew fresher, sending the fleet along at 7 knots; it so continued on the eleventh, with a heavy following sea. But signs of land, such as branches of trees with green leaves and flowers, became so frequent that the people were content with their Captain General's decision, and the mutinous mutterings died out in the keen anticipation of making a landfall in the Indies.

As the sun set under a clear horizon October 11, the northeast trade breezed up to gale force, and the three ships tore along at 9 knots. But Columbus refused to shorten sail, since his promised time was running out. He signaled everyone to keep a particularly sharp watch, and offered extra rewards for first landfall in addition to the year's pay promised by the Sovereigns. That night of destiny was clear and beautiful with a late rising moon, but the sea was the roughest of the entire passage. The men were tense and expectant, the officers testy and anxious, the Captain General serene in the confidence that presently God would reveal to him the promised Indies.

At 10 P.M., an hour before moonrise, Columbus and a seaman, almost simultaneously, thought they saw a light "like a little wax candle rising and falling." Others said they saw it too, but most did not; and after a few minutes it disappeared. Volumes have been written to explain what this light was or might have been. To a seaman it requires no explanation. It was an illusion, created by overtense watchfulness. When uncertain of your exact position, and straining to make a night landfall, you are apt to see imaginary lights and flashes and to hear nonexistent bells and breakers.

On rush the ships, pitching, rolling, throwing spray — white waves at their bows and white wakes reflecting the moon. *Pinta* is perhaps half a mile in the lead, *Santa María* on her port quarter, *Niña* on the other side. Now one, now another forges ahead, but they are all making the greatest speed of which they are capable. With the sixth glass of the night watch, the last sands are running out of an era that began with the dawn of history. A few minutes now and destiny will turn up a glass the flow of whose sands we are still watching. Not since the birth of Christ has there been a night so full of meaning for the human race.

At 2 A.M., October 12, Rodrigo de Triana, lookout on *Pinta*, sees something like a white cliff shining in the moonlight, and sings out, *Tierra! tierra!* "Land! land!" Captain Pinzón verifies the landfall, fires a gun as agreed, and shortens sail to allow the flagship to catch up. As *Santa María* approaches, the Captain General

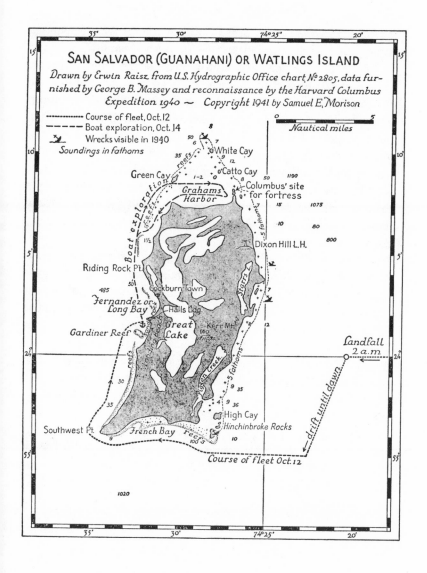

SAN SALVADOR (GUANAHANI) OR WATLINGS ISLAND

Drawn by Erwin Raisz from U.S. Hydrographic Office chart N° 2805, data furnished by George B. Massey and reconnaissance by the Harvard Columbus Expedition 1940 ~ Copyright 1941 by Samuel E. Morison

··············· Course of fleet, Oct.12
– – – – – Boat exploration, Oct.14
⚓ Wrecks visible in 1940
Soundings in fathoms

Nautical miles

8

White Cay

Catto Cay

Green Cay

Grahams Harbor

Columbus' site for fortress

Dixon Hill L.H.

Riding Rock Pt.

Cockburn Town

Fernandez or Long Bay

Hall's Ldg.

Gardiner Reef

Great Lake

Kerr Mt.

Landfall 2 a.m

Southwest Pt.

French Bay

High Cay

Hinchinbroke Rocks

drift until dawn

Course of fleet Oct.12

shouts across the rushing waters, "Señor Martín Alonso, you *did* find land! Five thousand maravedis for you as a bonus!"

Yes, land it was this time, a little island of the Bahamas group. The fleet was headed for the sand cliffs on its windward side and would have been wrecked had it held course. But these seamen were too expert to allow that to happen. The Captain General ordered sail to be shortened and the fleet to jog off and on until daylight, which was equivalent to a southwesterly drift clear of the island. At dawn they made full sail, passed the southern point of the island and sought an opening on the west coast, through the barrier reef. Before noon they found it, sailed into the shallow bay now called Long or Fernandez, and anchored in the lee of the land, in five fathoms.

Here on a gleaming beach of white coral occurred the famous first landing of Columbus. The Captain General (now by general consent called Admiral) went ashore in the flagship's boat with the royal standard of Castile displayed, the two Captains Pinzón in their boats, flying the banner of the Expedition — the green crowned cross on a white field. "And, all having rendered thanks to Our Lord, kneeling on the ground, embracing it with tears of joy for the immeasurable mercy of having reached it, the Admiral rose and gave this island the name *San Salvador*" — Holy Saviour.[2]

---

[2] Although there is still some difference of opinion, the generally accepted identification of Columbus's island is the one formerly called Watlings. It has been officially renamed San Salvador.

CHAPTER VII

Asia, or What?

THE NATIVES of Guanahaní, as they called this island, fled to the jungle when they saw three marine monsters approaching, but curiosity was too much for them, and when they peered out and saw strangely dressed human beings coming ashore, they approached timidly, with propitiatory gifts. Columbus, of course, had to believe that he was in the Indies, so he called these people "Indians," and Indians the native inhabitants of the Americas have become in all European languages.

Those first encountered were of the Taino branch of the Arawak language group. Coming from the mainland in dugout canoes, and with no better weapons than wooden spears, they had wrested the Bahamas and most of Cuba from the more primitive Siboney, within the previous century. The Tainos grew corn, yams and other roots for food; they knew how to make cassava bread, to spin and weave cotton and to make pottery. The Spaniards observed with wonder their fine build and almost complete nakedness, and noted with keen interest that some of them wore, suspended from the nose, little pendants of pure gold. The guilelessness and generosity of these children of nature — "they invite you to share anything that they possess, and show as much love as if their hearts went with it," wrote Columbus — their ignorance of money and of iron, and their nudity, suggested to every educated European that these people were holdovers from the Golden Age. Peter Martyr, first historian of the New World, wrote, "They seem to live in that golden world of the which old writers speak so much, wherein men lived simply and innocently without enforcement of laws, without quarreling, judges and libels, content only to satisfy nature." Columbus would much rather have encountered sophisticated Orientals than "noble savages," but as usual he made the best of the situation. He observed "how easy it would be to convert these people — and to make them work for us." In other words, enslave them but save their souls. Indeed, it seems to have been from the sailors who returned from this voyage that every Spaniard got the idea that no white man need do a hand's turn of work in the New World — God had provided docile natives to labor for the lords of creation.

For two days Columbus explored San Salvador. It was a pretty island then, with a heavy covering of tropical hardwood, but the Admiral knew full well that, interesting as the discovery of a new island and Golden Age natives might be, he had to bring home certain evidence of Japan or China, or plenty of gold and spices, to prove his voyage a success. The natives of San Salvador indicated by sign language that scores of islands lay to the west and south; it seemed to Columbus that these must be the ones shown on his chart, lying south of Cipangu, and that if they did not lead him to golden Japan, they would prove to be steppingstones to China.

So, detaining six Indians as guides, Columbus shoved off on the afternoon of October 14. That day he discovered another island which he named Santa María de la Concepción — the English prosaically called it Rum Cay. The natives proved to be similar in every respect to those on San Salvador and were equally pleased with the Admiral's gifts of red caps, glass beads and hawks' bells. That standard trading truck for the African coast proved equally saleworthy in the Antilles, especially the hawks' bells. These were little spherical bells about the diameter of a quarter dollar or shill-

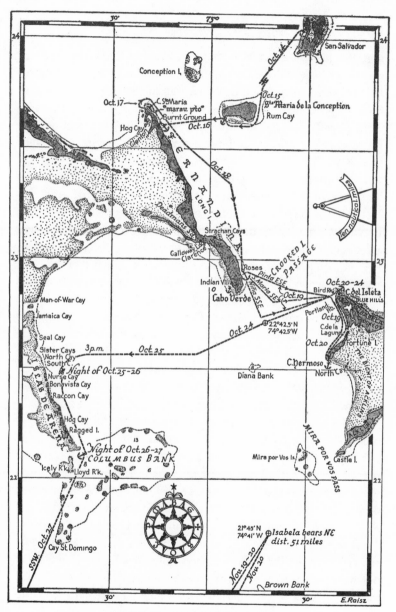

COURSE OF COLUMBUS'S
FLEET THROUGH THE BAHAMAS

ing, which were attached to the birds used in falconry; they had a pleasant little tinkle like a miniature sleighbell, and the natives loved them. Indians would paddle out to the flagship, waggling their fingers and saying, *Chuq! chuq!* meaning, "More hawks' bells, please!" Lace points, the metal tips to the laces then used to fasten men's clothing, and brass tambourine jingles also were favorites.

The Admiral's native guides, eager to please, kept assuring him by signs that in the next island there would be plenty of gold, but each one in succession — Long Island, Crooked Island, Fortune Island — proved to be no different from San Salvador. Each was a flat, jungle-covered bit of land inhabited by friendly natives who had no gold except for a few ornaments which they had obtained elsewhere. Where they got them he could never make out, because of the language barrier; De Torres, the interpreter, found his Arabic no use whatsoever. Columbus saw the first maize or Indian corn ever observed by a European, the first hammocks, woven from native cotton, and the first yams and sweet potatoes; also, a tree that he estimated correctly would prove to be good dye wood. But no sign of gold except on the natives' persons.

As the Admiral and his Indian guides came to understand each other better, he heard about a big island that they called Colba (Cuba) and made up his mind that it must be either Japan or a part of China. So to Colba he must go, and the Indians took him there by their usual canoe route, so laid out as to be the shortest possible jump over blue water. They sailed across Crooked Island Passage to the line of cays at the southeast edge of the Great Bahama Bank. From Ragged Island, on October 27, the fleet made a fast sail over the shoals now named Columbus Bank, with a fresh northeast wind, to where the Indians pointed out "Colba." And on the morning of October 28 they entered Bahía Bariay, in the

Cuban Province of Oriente. Columbus observed in his Journal that he had never seen so beautiful a harbor — trees all fair and green and different from ours, some with bright flowers and some heavy with fruit, and the air full of birdsong. But where was the evidence of Japan? Where the golden-roofed temples, the dragon-mouthed bronze cannon, the lords and ladies in gold-stiffened brocade?

Poor Columbus! He tried so hard to find compensation in the strange new things he did see for the Oriental objects he so much wanted to see, but it was difficult to describe the scenery, flora and inhabitants of Cuba in such wise as to interest important people in Spain. Nor could he be hospitable to the teasing thought that this was not the Orient after all, but a new world.

Next day the three ships sailed westward along the many-harbored coast of Cuba, Columbus hoping every moment to meet a welcoming fleet of Chinese junks, and anchored in Puerto Gibara. There they remained for twelve days, except for a brief jaunt westward to Punta Cobarrubia and back.

As the San Salvador interpreters assured the local Indians that the strangers in the white-winged monsters were fine people, with piles of good trading truck, business for a time was brisk. Anxious to please, they told Columbus that there was gold in the interior, at a place called Cubanacan, which meant mid-Cuba. The Admiral, eager to present his letter of introduction to the Chinese Emperor, mistook this for *El Gran Can,* the Great Khan. So nothing would do but to send an embassy to Cubanacan. Luis de Torres, the Arabic scholar, was in charge and second in command was Rodrigo de Xeres, an able seaman who had once met a Negro king in Guinea and so was supposed to know the proper way to approach pagan royalty. Indians carried the diplomatic portfolio (Latin passport and royal letter of credence to the Grand Khan), a gift considered suitable for royalty, and strings of glass beads to buy food from the natives. The embassy tramped up the valley of the Cacoyuguin River, past fields cultivated with corn, beans and sweet potatoes, to what they hoped would be Cambaluk, the imperial city where the Great Khan resided. Alas, it was a village of about fifty palm-thatched huts, on the site of the present town of Holguín. The two Spaniards, regarded as having come from the sky, were feasted by the local cacique, while the populace swarmed up to kiss their feet and present simple gifts. Rodrigo the sailor loved it — he had never had it so good in Africa — but Torres was mortified that his Arabic was not understood, and, expecting a reception by mandarins in a stone-built capital of ten thousand houses, he felt very much let down.

Yet, on their way back to the harbor, the embassy made a discovery which (had they only known it) would have more far-reaching results in human happiness than any possible treaty with China. As Columbus records it, they met "many people who were going to their villages, with a firebrand in the hand, and herbs to drink the smoke thereof, as they are accustomed." You have guessed it, reader; this was the first European contact with tobacco. The Tainos used it in the form of cigars (which they called *tobacos*); a walking party, such as the embassy encountered, would carry a large cigar and at every halt light it from a firebrand; everyone then took three or four "drags" from it through his nostrils; and after all were refreshed, the march was resumed, small boys keeping the firebrand alight until the next stop. Not long after Spaniards settled in the New World, they tried smoking tobacco and liked it, and through them its use spread rapidly through Europe, Asia and Africa.

While the embassy was absent, Columbus totted up his dead reckoning and figured that he had made 90 degrees of westing. This, owing to his overestimate of the length of Asia, should put the ships right where China began. He decided that Cuba was the "Province of Mangi," a name which the more or less imaginative maps of China that he had seen placed on a peninsula at the southeast corner of the Empire. The Admiral also tried to shoot the North Star with his primitive quadrant. Unfortunately, he picked the wrong star, Alfirk of the constellation Cepheus, which on that November evening hung directly over Polaris, and so found Cuba to be in latitude 42 degrees North, the latitude of Cape Cod! Of course he knew that this was wrong, since he had sailed across on 28 degrees North, and in his Letter on this voyage he corrected the latitude of northern Cuba to 26 degrees, still 5 degrees too much.

The Admiral began a collection of specimens which he hoped would convince people at home that he was at least on the fringe of Asia. There was a shrub which smelled something like cinnamon, and so must be cinnamon; the gumbo-limbo, which he supposed to be an Asiatic form of the gum mastic that he had seen in Chios; and the small, inedible *nogal del país*, which he identified as the coconut mentioned by Marco Polo. Coconut palms are such a feature of the Caribbean coast today that we forget that they, like the banana, were introduced by the Spaniards. The men dug up some roots which Maestro Sánchez, the surgeon, pronounced to be Chinese rhubarb, a valuable drug imported into Europe, but it turned out to be something different, not even as valuable as the humble pieplant.

And no gold as yet. When the Spaniards asked for gold, the Indians always waved them on to some other place. According to them, there was an island called Babeque where the people gathered gold on the beach by candlelight and hammered it into bars. This choice piece of misinformation brought about the first rift in the Spanish high command. Without asking the Admiral's permission, Martín Alonso Pinzón took off in *Pinta*, hoping to be the first to reach Babeque. He called at Great Inagua Island, which lay in the general direction indicated by the Indians, and, needless to say, found no gold by candle or any other light.

The Admiral in *Santa María*, with *Niña* (whose captain, Vicente Yáñez Pinzón, remained always loyal), sailed eastward along the superb coast of the Oriente Province. Noble mountains rise directly from the sea, but every few miles there is a river whose mouth makes a good landlocked harbor. He called at Bahía Tánamo with its bottle-neck entrance and, within, little wooded islands running up "like diamond points," and others flat-topped "like tables." Next, he put in at the beautiful Puerto Cayo Moa, where you have to pick an opening through the breakers and then find yourself, as Columbus said, in "a lagoon in which all the ships of Spain could lie and be safe." The peculiar charm of this placid harbor, so calm between lofty mountains and the barrier of foaming reefs, was noted by Columbus in words that are not in the least exaggerated. He had an eye, too, for practical matters, and when the men rowed him up the river mouth, he observed on the mountain slopes pine trees which he said would make timber for the Spanish Navy. The descendants of those pines are now being sawed at a mill run by the mountain stream whose distant roar Columbus heard on a Sunday in November, 1492.

On he sailed, with a breeze that fortunately came from the west, noting no less than nine little harbors, behind which leafy valleys ran up into the lofty sierra. He passed the anvil-shaped mountain El Yunque, landmark for Baracoa, a harbor which Columbus well described as round "like a little porringer." Here, a proper site for a colony, the first Spanish settlement in Cuba was pitched in 1512, but Baracoa afforded no gold, and the fleet passed on as soon as the wind turned fair. At sunrise December 5 it was off Cape Maisí, easternmost point of Cuba. In the hope that this was the extremity of Asia, corresponding to Cape St. Vincent in Europe, Columbus named it Cape Alpha and Omega, where East ends and West begins.

Now the fleet crossed the Windward Passage, and at nightfall arrived off the Haitian harbor of San Nicolás Môle, so named by Columbus because he entered it on the feast day of that favorite saint of children. His Indian guides had indicated that gold was to be found on this great island, the home of their ancestors, and this time they were right. It may be said that this island saved Columbus's reputation, for if he had returned home with no more "evidence" than he had yet obtained, people would have said, "This Genoese has found some interesting savage islands, inhabited by gentle natives of the Golden Age, but as for their being the Indies — pooh!"

Nimble *Niña* got into harbor that night, but *Santa María* sailed an offshore leg with the land breeze, in order to be in a good windward position to enter San Nicolás next morning. At daylight the Admiral took a four-point fix on Cape San Nicolás Môle, the Island of Tortuga and two Haitian capes to the eastward, so accurately that we can pinpoint his position on a modern chart.

A fair breeze took the two vessels to Moustique Bay, where they were detained five days by easterly winds and rain. It was here that the Admiral, "seeing the grandeur and beauty of this island, and its resemblance to the land of Spain," named it La Isla Española, The Spanish Isle.[1] Three of his seamen captured a young and beautiful girl clad only in a golden nose plug, and brought her on board. The Admiral "sent her ashore very honorably," decently clad in slop-chest clothing and bedecked with jingles and hawks'

---

[1] On official charts it is called Hispaniola, to obviate confusion between the two republics into which the island is divided, the Dominican and the Haitian.

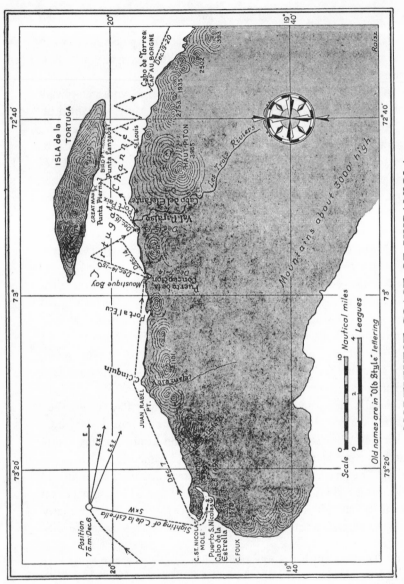

NORTHWEST COAST OF HISPANIOLA

bells, although she indicated that she would rather stay with the boys. This move proved to be useful for public relations, as the damsel was a cacique's daughter. Next day nine Spaniards who followed a trail were conducted to a big village of one or two thousand people and given everything they wanted — food, drink, parrots and girls.

On December 15 the two ships beat up the Tortuga Channel to the mouth of Trois Rivières, a clear mountain stream that flows through a valley that Columbus well named the Valley of Paradise. Next day, when the fleet lay off a beach, some five hundred people came down, accompanied by their youthful cacique, who made the Admiral a state visit. Columbus had not been much impressed by a cacique who came on board in Cuba, but this one was different. He had dinner alone with the Admiral in his cabin, and behaved himself with royal poise and dignity. Moreover, he and his suite were bedecked with solid-gold jewelry! Columbus had the cacique piped over the side in proper naval style and given a twenty-one-gun salute. Again the thought passed through his mind that these people were ripe for exploitation — "very cowardly," and "fit to be ordered about and made to work, to sow and do aught else that may be needed." A wonderful chance, he observed, for his Sovereigns, whose subjects were not notably fond of hard work!

At sunrise December 20, the ships were off Acul Bay, the beauty of which was so striking that the Admiral ran out of adjectives describing it. Acul certainly is one of the most beautiful bays in the world. The high mountains part to reveal a conical peak at the head of the valley, which for the last 150 years has been crowned by the stone citadel of Henri Christophe, King of Haiti. Here the natives, in 1492, were in an even more pristine state of innocence than elsewhere; the women did not even wear a scanty cotton clout, and the men did not mind exhibiting their wives and daughters to the strangers. Also, they seemed to have plenty of gold. Every day the Spaniards' appetite for the precious metal was being whetted.

During the night of December 22–23, and the following morning, about a thousand people came out in canoes to visit *Santa María,* and some five hundred more swam out, although she was anchored over three miles from the nearest shore. After Indians and white men had taken each others' measure, any such promiscuous visiting would not have been allowed, lest the natives capture the ships, but no such thought now crossed the minds of these gentle Tainos.

A messenger arrived at Acul from Guacanagarí, the cacique of Marien, the northwestern part of Haiti, and a more important potentate than the one entertained a few days earlier. Guacanagarí sent the Admiral a magnificent belt with a solid-gold mask for buckle, and invited him to call. He needed no second invitation, since everyone assured him the gold mines were in that direction, and that the central part of the island was called Cibao, which suggested Cipangu, Japan. So, before sunrise on December 24, *Santa María* and *Niña* departed Acul Bay, all hands planning to spend a merry Christmas at the court of Guacanagarí, who might even turn out to be the Emperor of Japan!

Fate decreed otherwise. With a contrary wind, the two vessels were unable to cover the few miles between Acul and Guacanagarí's capital on Caracol Bay in a day. By 11 P.M., when the watch was changed, *Niña* and *Santa María* were becalmed east of Cape Haitien, inside the Limonade Pass to the barrier reef. Every one on board was exhausted from the previous all-night entertainment of natives, and as the water was calm, with only a slight ground swell and no wind, a feeling of complete security — the most dangerous delusion a seaman can entertain — stole over the flagship. Even the Admiral retired to get his first sleep in forty-eight hours; the helmsman gave the big tiller to a small boy and joined the rest of the watch in slumber.

Just as midnight ushered in Christmas Day, *Santa María* settled on a coral reef, so gently that nobody was awakened by the shock. The boy helmsman, feeling the rudder ground, sang out; the Admiral was first on deck, followed by Captain La Cosa and all hands. As the bow only had grounded, Columbus saw a good chance to get her off stern first and ordered La Cosa and a boat's crew to run an anchor out astern. Instead of obeying orders, they rowed to *Niña*. Captain Vicente Pinzón refused to receive them and sent a boat of his own to help. *Niña,* which was either more vigilant than the flagship or not on the same bearing, had passed the reef safely.

Owing to La Cosa's cowardice or insubordination, an hour was wasted, and that doomed *Santa María.* The ground swell had been driving her higher and higher on the reef, and coral heads were punching holes in her bottom. As the hull was filling with water, Columbus ordered abandon ship, hoping that daylight would make it easier to float her. And the tide, though only a few inches might help.

Guacanagarí and his subjects worked hard with the Spaniards to get her off after daybreak, but it was too late. All they could salvage were the equipment, stores and trading truck, which the Indians faithfully guarded and (so the Admiral recorded) purloined not so much as a lace point.

Columbus, with his strong sense of divine guidance, tried to figure out what this strange and apparently disastrous accident meant. Presently he had it: God intended him to start a colony at that point, with *Santa María's* crew. Guacanagarí begged him to do so, as he wanted fire power to help him against enemies elsewhere on the island. The Spaniards fell over each other to volunteer, because signs of gold were now so plentiful that they were confident of making their fortunes. So Columbus gave orders to erect a fortified camp ashore and named it Villa de la Navidad (Christmas Town) in honor of the day of disaster, which he fondly thought had been turned to his advantage.

Navidad, the first attempt by Europeans since that of the Northmen to establish themselves in the New World, was soon built. It was probably located on the sandspit now called Limonade Bord-de-Mer, off which there is good anchorage. The fort was constructed largely out of *Santa María's* timbers. Thirty-nine men, mostly from the flagship but some from *Niña*, were left behind under command of Columbus's Cordovan friend Diego de Harana. The Admiral gave them a good part of his provisions, most of the trading truck and the flagship's boat. They were instructed to explore the country with a view to finding a permanent settlement, to trade for gold and to treat the natives kindly.

Columbus was now certain that he had found the Indies. Hispaniola might not be Japan, but it was a great and rich island off the coast of China, with a population ripe both for conversion and exploitation. He now had enough gold artifacts to convince the most skeptical that a land of wealth and plenty had been discovered.

On the day after New Year's, 1493, Guacanagarí and Columbus held a farewell party. *Niña* fired gunshots through what was left of the hull of *Santa María* to impress the natives, and the cacique feasted all hands. After final expressions of mutual love and esteem, and warm embraces, the new allies parted, and the Admiral went on board *Niña*. He would return home in her, with *Pinta* if he could find her; otherwise, alone. After a wait for a favorable wind, and for shipmates who had overstayed their leave, she set sail at sunrise January 4, and the homeward passage began.

CHAPTER VIII

Homeward Passage

WHEN HE DEPARTED Navidad, Columbus intended to shape a course directly for Spain, lest Pinzón get there first with the good news. But two days later he sighted *Pinta* sailing from the other direction, down wind. That evening Martín Alonso came on board and gave a fairly convincing account of his doings during the last three weeks. He had called at the Great Inagua, ascertained that the yarn about picking up gold by candlelight was a myth, then sailed along the coast of Hispaniola and anchored in Puerto Blanco. There a shore party penetrated the Cibao and found plenty of gold. Pinzón had heard of the flagship's wreck by Indian "grapevine" and had decided to sail back and lend the Admiral a hand. Columbus was inclined to let bygones be bygones in view of the good news of gold, and he was pleased to have company on the voyage home. Nobody in that era sailed on a long voyage unescorted if he could help it.

While waiting for a fair wind to double Monte Cristi peninsula, behind which they were anchored, Columbus explored the lower course of the Rio Yaque del Norte and found gold nuggets as large as lentils. Even today there is gold in that river valley; the country women pan it out laboriously, and when they have enough to fill a turkey quill, they take it to town for their shopping.

At midnight January 8 *Niña* and *Pinta* resumed the homeward passage. Passing along the coast of Hispaniola, they looked in at

Puerto Plata (so named by Columbus on account of silver clouds over the mountains) and anchored near the mouth of Samaná Bay, where the United States later contemplated establishing a naval base. There, at a place still called the Point of the Arrows, the Spaniards encountered the first natives armed with bows and arrows and who were not pleased to meet them. These were a branch of the Tainos called Ciguayos, who in self-defense against raiding Caribs from Puerto Rico had adopted their weapons. By dint of catching one Ciguayo, treating him well and sending him ashore with an assortment of red cloth and trinkets, the rest were appeased, and a brisk if somewhat cautious trade was conducted. Also, one or two were persuaded to join the native contingent returning to Spain.

On Wednesday, January 16, three hours before daybreak, the caravels sailed from Samaná Bay. A rough voyage lay ahead, and a very difficult problem in navigation. This homeward passage was a far greater test of Columbus's courage and seamanship and ability to handle men than anything he had hitherto experienced. With the greatest geographical discovery of all time locked in his breast, knowing that it would be of no use to anybody unless delivered, the Admiral had to fight the elements and human weakness as never before or since.

Before heading for home, Columbus intended to check an Amazonian myth of the Tainos about Matinino, the later Martinique. They told him that this island was inhabited only by Carib women, who received an annual male visitation but got rid of the men as soon as they had accomplished what they came for. The myth probably arose from the fact that Carib women fought beside their men, or alone if the men were absent. Columbus was not moved so much by curiosity as wishing to gather more Oriental evidence, because Marco Polo had told a tall tale about "Islands Masculina and Feminea" in the Indian Ocean, and they are depicted on Behaim's globe. However, the intended call on the Amazons was canceled when the wind came west — unusual for that place and season. The Admiral thought it was too good a chance to miss, and decided to sail directly to Spain.

The west wind soon petered out, the easterly trades returned, and the caravels sailed as best they could, close-hauled on the starboard tack. Modern sailing craft can sail as close to the wind as four points (45 degrees) or, if very smart racers in smooth water, even closer. *Niña* and *Pinta* could lay up to five points (56 degrees) if the sea was smooth, but under ordinary conditions could not do better than six points (67½ degrees), and *Pinta* was slow on the wind, owing to a sprung mizzenmast. This meant, in practice, that if it blew from the southeast, the caravels could steer east-northeast; with a due east wind the best course toward Spain of which they were capable was north-northeast; and if it backed to northeast (as the trade wind often does), the Admiral had to bring them about on the port tack and steer east-southeast.

In this manner *Niña* and *Pinta* continued through January, constantly reaching farther north and edging a little closer to Spain. As they were near the northern limit of the trades, the sea was smooth and, providentially, the wind held and blew them across the horse latitudes, as seamen used to call the calms between latitudes 30 and 33 degrees North. They successfully crossed the Sargasso Sea, having the rare experience of sailing with a fresh wind across an undulating meadow of gulfweed, under a full moon. That is indeed beautiful to the eye, and to the ear, too, as the sound of parting waters is replaced by a soft "hush-hush" as the weed brushes by. Without knowing it, Columbus had employed the best sailing strategy for getting home quickly. If he had tried to sail straight to Spain (as on his return passage in 1496), he would have had to beat to windward most of the way, but this long northerly leg took him up to the latitude of Bermuda into the zone of rough, strong westerlies.

On the last day of January the wind swung into the west, and four days later, when the Admiral figured by a simple "eye sight" of the North Star that he had reached latitude 37 degrees North (that of Cape St. Vincent) and actually was in that of Gibraltar, he set the course due east. This, owing to compass variation, was actually about 80 degrees true, which happened to be right for picking up the Azores. The weather now turned cold and a fresh gale blew up. For four days the caravels made an average of 150 miles, and during one twenty-four-hour period almost 200 miles, at times attaining a speed of eleven knots.

When any sailing yacht the length of *Niña* and *Pinta* hits it up to eleven or twelve knots today, it is something to talk about, and these caravels were having the finest kind of sailing. They were running before a fresh gale over deep blue, white-crested water. On they sped through bright, sunny days and nights brilliant with Orion and other familiar constellations that seemed to be beckoning them home. It is hard for any sailor to be sorry for Columbus, in spite of his later misfortunes; he enjoyed such glorious sailing weather on almost every voyage. But he had some very tough experiences, and one of the worst was about to come.

By nightfall February 7 the westerly gale died down, and for two days the caravels had light variables and made little progress. On the ninth they were able to square away again eastward. Next day the pilots and captains held a ship-to-ship discussion of their position. Everyone, including Columbus, thought they were much farther south than they actually were, and all except the Admiral put them on the meridian of the eastern Azores; but Columbus estimated correctly that they were almost due south of Flores, and decided to call at one of the Azores, if possible.

He almost didn't make it. The two caravels were sailing into an area of very dirty weather in one of the coldest and most blustery winters on record — a winter in which hundreds of vessels were wrecked, the harbor of Genoa froze over, and ships lay windbound at Lisbon for months. The center of an area of very low pressure was passing north of the Azores with southwest to west winds of full gale strength (force 9 to 10 on Beaufort scale), and the caravels had to pass through three weather fronts.

On February 12, *Niña* stripped down to bare poles and scudded before the wind, laboring heavily. The wind moderated slightly next morning, then increased, and *Niña* ran into frightful cross seas. The isobaric system was elongated, as in hurricane "Edna" of 1954, which is raging as I write. This brought opposite winds very close to one another. The resulting cross seas formed dangerous pyramidical waves that broke over the caravels from stem to stern, and *Niña* was underballasted, owing to the depletion of her stores. With only her reefed main course set, and the yard slung low, she sailed in a general northeasterly direction, while the Admiral and Captain Vicente Pinzón took turns as officer of the deck and watched each wave to warn the helmsman below. One mistake by either and she would have broached-to, rolled over and sunk, and *Pinta* could never have rescued survivors in such a sea.

The following night, February 13–14, the two caravels lost sight of each other and never met again until they reached harbor in Spain. And they almost did not get there. We have no record of how *Pinta* fared, but *Niña's* crew almost gave up hope on St. Valentine's Day. Thrice, officers and men drew lots for one to go on a pilgrimage to some famous shrine if they were saved; but the wind only blew harder. Then all made a vow "to go in procession in their shirts" to the first shrine of the Virgin they might encounter. The wind then began to abate. Columbus afterwards admitted that he was as frightened as anyone. Desperate lest both ships and all hands perish, at the height of the gale he wrote in ink on a parchment an abstract of his journal of the voyage, wrapped it in waxed cloth, headed it up in a cask and hove it overboard in the hope that someone might pick up the true story of his discovery. The cask never was recovered, but sundry faked-up versions of the Admiral's "Secrete Log Boke" are still being offered to credulous collectors.

Shortly after sunrise February 15, land was sighted dead ahead. Columbus correctly guessed that it was one of the Azores; which one he did not know. And as the wind then whipped into the east, three days elapsed before *Niña* was able to come up with this island and anchor. The Admiral sent his boat ashore and ascertained that it was Santa Maria, southernmost of the Azores. He had anchored near a village called Nossa Senhora dos Anjos (Our Lady of the Angels), where a little church was dedicated to the Virgin, who had made an appearance, surrounded by angels, to a local fisherman. Anjos was an answer to prayer, and the proper place for the crew to fulfill their vow made at the height of the storm.

There then took place what, in retrospect, seems the most comic incident of the entire First Voyage. Here were men bursting with the greatest piece of news since the fall of the Roman Empire, a discovery that would confer untold benefits on Europe and Europeans; yet, what was their first reception? While saying their prayers in the little chapel, clad only in their shirts (as a sign of penitence), half the crew were set upon by "the whole town" and thrown into jail. The Portuguese captain of the island suspected that they had been on an illicit voyage to West Africa! He even rowed out to capture Columbus and the few members of *Niña's* crew who had stayed on board, intending to make their pilgrimage later. The Admiral refused to receive him and threatened to shoot up the town and carry off hostages if his people were not released. Before the captain could make up his mind, another storm blew up, *Niña's* cables parted, and she was blown almost to São Miguel and back. And she did well to get back, because only three seamen and the Indians were left on board to help the Admiral and the skipper. By the time *Niña* returned, the Portuguese captain, having grilled the captured sailors and discovered no evidence of poaching on his King's preserves, surrendered them and furnished the entire crew with much needed fresh provisions.

So on February 24 Columbus resumed his homeward voyage. The distance to his desired landfall, Cape St. Vincent, was only 800 miles, which should have required only a week's sail in the prevailing north wind. But this piece of ocean in winter is a place where low-pressure areas hang around and make trouble for poor sailors, and the winter of 1493 was unusually foul. Another tempest overtook *Niña* about 250 miles from Santa Maria and stayed with her all the way. Two cyclones were moving slowly eastward, taking six days to pass *Niña*, and giving her an even worse beating than did the storm west of the Azores.

Trouble began on February 26. The wind shifted to southeast, forcing *Niña* to change course to east-northeast. "It was painful," wrote Columbus, "to have such a tempest when they were already at the doors of home." Next day both wind and sea made up, and for three days more they were blown off their course. On the night of March 2 the warm front of the circular storm hit *Niña*, the wind changed to southwest, and she was able to sail her course, but that same night the cold front overtook her with a violent squall which split the main course and blew the furled forecourse and mizzen out of their gaskets, whipping them to ragged ribbons in a few minutes. So Columbus did the only thing he could do; he drove on under bare poles. *Niña* pitched and rolled frightfully in cross seas and the wind made another shift, to northwest, on March 3. This was the "backlash" of the cyclone, and, as in the hurricane that hit New England on September 11, 1954, it was worse than the forelash. As the dark winter afternoon waned, anxiety became intense. Columbus and the pilots knew by dead reckoning that they were driving right onto the ironbound coast of Portugal, and that only a miracle could prevent a smash-up against the cliffs.

Shortly after six o'clock, when the sun set, the crisis came. Lightning flashed overhead, great seas broke aboard from both sides, the wind blew so strong it "seemed to raise the caravel into the air." Fortunately it was the night of full moon, which sent enough light through the clouds so that at seven o'clock land was sighted dead ahead, distant perhaps five miles. Columbus then performed the difficult maneuver, well known to every old-time seaman, of "clawing off" a lee shore. The coast ran north and south, the wind was northwest, so they set one little square fore-sail that had been saved in the locker, wore ship in a smother of foam, and shaped a course south, parallel to the coast, with wind on the starboard quarter. No wonder *Niña* became the Admiral's favorite vessel, to stand all that beating and respond to this difficult maneuver without broaching.

When day broke on March 4, Columbus recognized prominent Cape Roca, that juts into the ocean from the mountains of Sintra, just north of the entrance to the Tagus. With only one square sail between him and utter destruction, the Admiral naturally elected to enter the Tagus and call at Lisbon to refit rather than attempt to continue around Cape St. Vincent to Spain. He knew perfectly well that he was taking a big risk in placing himself in the power of King John II, the ruthless monarch who had turned him down twice, but his first and second considerations — probably in that order — were to get the word of his discovery to Spain and to save his ship and crew. So, after sunrise, *Niña* whipped around Cape Roca, passed Cascais, where the fishermen were amazed to see so tiny a vessel coming in from sea, crossed the smoking bar at the river mouth, and by nine o'clock anchored off Belém, the outer port of Lisbon.

To be safely anchored in a snug harbor after long tossing at sea gives the sailor a wonderful feeling of relief and relaxation. But the Admiral and his battered crew still had plenty to worry about. *Niña* would have to be refitted before she could proceed to Spain, and would King John allow it? And what had happened to *Pinta?*

The first Portuguese gesture was not assuring. Moored near *Niña* was a large warship whose master was Bartholomew Dias, discoverer of the Cape of Good Hope, and whose captain was a well-known officer of the royal navy. Before long, Dias came over in an armed boat and ordered Captain Colom (as he knew Columbus) to report on board the warship and give an account of himself. Columbus stood on his dignity as Admiral of the Ocean Sea, and refused. But he showed his credentials, which satisfied both Dias and the captain, who boarded *Niña* on a visit of courtesy, "with drums, trumpets and pipes," and offered to procure any provisions or chandlery that the Admiral needed. Columbus had already sent a letter to King John, asking permission to enter the port of Lisbon, and on March 8 a nobleman brought the answer, which not only granted his request and ordered that *Niña* be supplied with all she needed, gratis, but invited the Admiral to visit the King at his country residence. Columbus decided he had better accept, although it meant another delay, and he feared lest making a visit to the King of Portugal before reporting to Queen Isabella would offend her; as indeed it did. So, selecting two or three followers and some of the healthiest of his captive Indians, Columbus landed at Lisbon and chartered a train of mules to take himself and suite upcountry. Pity the poor Indians who, after their terrible buffeting at sea, must now suffer the rigors of muleback transport along the narrow, muddy roads of Portugal! It took them two days to make the thirty-mile journey to the monastery of Santa Maria das Virtudes, where the King was then staying.

John II received Columbus with unexpected graciousness, but his court chronicler tells us that the King was inwardly furious with the Admiral for telling what sounded like a tall tale, and he suspected that the new discoveries had been made in a region where Portugal had prior rights. The courtiers urged the King to have this boastful upstart discreetly assassinated (just as he had recently disposed of an annoying brother-in-law), but, fortunately, he refused. And the King had to admit that his Indian guests looked very different from any Africans he had ever seen or heard of. Two of them impressed him deeply by making a rough chart of the Antilles with beans, at which the King was convinced, smote his breast and cried out, "Why did I let slip such a wonderful chance?"

These Indians really were remarkable geographers. They told Columbus, who repeated it in his Letter on the First Voyage, that an island named Matinino was the nearest island in the Caribbean to Spain, and that the second in order was Charis (Dominica). That is very close to the truth, and the Admiral, as we shall see, set a direct course for that strategic corner of the Lesser Antilles on his Second Voyage.

On March 11, Columbus and suite departed, escorted by a troop of cavaliers, and made a detour to call on the Queen of Portugal at the Convent of São Antonio de Castanheira. The Admiral was so sore from his muleback cruise that he left his cavalcade at Alhandra on the Tagus and there chartered a boat to take him down river to *Niña*. During his absence she had been fitted with a new suit of sails and running rigging, and had taken on fresh provisions, wood, water, and doubtless a cask of wine. She was now ready for the last leg of the voyage, all her crew were on board, and on the following morning, March 13, the gallant little caravel weighed anchor from Lisbon.

Strange to relate, *Pinta* was following her, out of sight but not far astern. She had missed the Azores and so was not subjected to the last and worst of the tempests that swept over *Niña*, and she made port at Bayona near Vigo in northern Spain about the end of February. Martín Alonso Pinzón, whom Columbus had suspected of wanting to beat him home with the news, attempted just that. He sent a message across Spain to Ferdinand and Isabella at Barcelona, announcing his arrival and begging permission to come himself and tell them all about the voyage. The Sovereigns sent back word that they preferred to hear the news from Columbus himself. *Pinta* then sailed from Bayona for Palos.

At daybreak, March 14, *Niña* wore ship around Cape St. Vincent and passed the beach where Columbus had swum ashore after the sea fight seventeen years earlier. And at midday, March 15, she crossed the bar of Rio Saltés on the young flood tide and dropped anchor off Palos.

Pinta entered on the same tide. The sight of *Niña* already there, snugged down as if she had been at home a month, finished Martín Alonso Pinzón. Older than Columbus, ill from the hardships of the voyage, mortified by his snub from the King and Queen, he could bear no more. He went directly from *Pinta* to his country house near Palos, took to his bed and died within the month.

So ended, 224 days after it began, the greatest round voyage in history. Columbus's final words to his Journal of it have been preserved:

Of this voyage I observe that the will of God hath miraculously been set forth (as may be seen from this journal) by the many signal miracles that He hath shown on the voyage and for myself, who for so great a time was in the court of Your Highnesses, with the opposition and against the opinion of so many high personages of your household, who were all against me, alleging this undertaking to be folly, which I hope in Our Lord will be to the greater glory of Christianity, which to some slight extent has already occurred.

Thus, even in the moment of his triumph, when his persistence, intuition and sea knowledge had received the divine accolade of success, Columbus could not resist lashing back at the fools, skeptics and men of learning who had derided or doubted him. Almost every pioneer in science or learning has to endure much before he can get his ideas across, and if he has no money and can do nothing without it, he must expect to be kept waiting and to experience ridicule, deceit, rudeness, pomposity and all kinds of opposition. But when he finally gets what he wants, and succeeds, he does well to keep quiet about all this, and even to congratulate those who doubted him for the help they failed to give. Columbus never learned to do so. He could hardly write one letter or report without derogatory comments on his detractors, which naturally made them eager to humble and degrade, rather than to honor and assist him.

CHAPTER IX
Hour of Triumph

COLUMBUS had already sent his official report on the voyage (generally called the Letter to Santangel, or simply the Columbus Letter) overland from Lisbon to Barcelona. Fearing lest it miscarry, or be impounded by King John II, he now sent one copy of it to the Sovereigns by official courier, and a third to the municipality at Cordova, where his mistress Beatriz was awaiting him with five-year-old Ferdinand and thirteen-year-old Diego. Before proceeding to Seville to await the reply, he performed his vows at the churches of Santa María de la Cinta at Huelva, and at Santa Clara (from whom *Niña* had been named) de Moguer near Palos, and spent two weeks with Fray Juan Pérez and his other friends at La Rábida. On Palm Sunday, March 31, he entered Seville just in time to take part in the traditional cere-monies of Holy Week.

On or shortly after Easter Sunday, April 7, his cup of happiness overflowed upon receipt of a letter from Ferdinand and Isabella, addressed to "Don Cristóbal Colón, their Admiral of the Ocean Sea, Viceroy and Governor of the Islands that he hath discovered in the Indies." These were the exact titles that they had promised him if he did reach the Indies, and the use of them indicated that they believed he had made good. They expressed their pleasure at his achievements, commanded him to attend court, and, "Inasmuch as we will that that which you have commenced with the aid of God be continued and furthered," ordered preparations for a second voyage to be started immediately.

Sweet words indeed! Columbus promptly drafted a report for the Sovereigns on how Hispaniola should be colonized. As chance entries in his Journal prove, he had been thinking this over for several months. The result was a modification of the trading-factory idea with which he had begun his First Voyage. He now proposed to recruit a maximum of two thousand settlers who would be required to build houses in a designated town in return for a license to trade with the natives of the interior for gold. Each one must return to his town at stated intervals and hand over his gold for smelting to an official who would deduct the Sovereigns' fifth, the Admiral's tenth, and another tax to support the church. There should be a closed season on gold-hunting in order to insure that the settlers would grow crops. Foreigners, Jews, infidels and heretics must be kept out of the Indies, but plenty of priests should be sent there to convert the natives.

Evidently Columbus had already realized from his contact with the Tainos that their wants were few and easily supplied, so that they could not be expected to flock to the beach to sell gold, as the natives of Africa did. Spaniards would have to work the interior of Hispaniola, and perhaps visit other islands as well, to do business. But everyone must check in at a trading factory on the coast, and all transatlantic traffic must go to and from Cadiz, in the interest of fiscal control.

After sending this report ahead by courier, the Admiral purchased clothes suitable for his rank and formed a procession with some of his officers, hired servants and six of the long-suffering Indians. These wore their native full dress (largely feathers and fishbone-and-gold ornaments) and carried parrots in cages. The news traveled ahead, and everyone who possibly could flocked to marvel at these strange-looking men, so unlike any in European experience. Traversing lovely Andalusia, they entered Cordova, where the municipality gave Columbus a great reception and he saw his mistress and picked up his two sons. Around April 20 the cavalcade arrived at Barcelona, where "all the court and the city" came out to meet the great man.

Now the fortunes of Columbus reached apogee. As he entered the hall where the Sovereigns held court, his dignified stature, his gray hair, and his noble countenance tanned by eight months on the sea made the learned men present compare him with a Roman senator. As he advanced to make obeisance, Ferdinand and Isabella rose from their thrones, and when he knelt to kiss their hands, they bade him rise and be seated on the Queen's right. The Indians were brought forward and presented, the gold artifacts and samples of alleged rare spices were examined, a multitude of questions asked and answered, then all adjourned to the chapel of the Alcazar where a *Te Deum* was chanted. And it was observed that at the last line, "O Lord, in Thee have I trusted, let me never be confounded," tears were streaming down the Admiral's face.

It is probable that Columbus at this point could have had anything he wanted — a title, castle in Spain, a pension for life and an endowment — and it would have been well for him had he then taken profits and retired with honor, leaving to others the responsibility of colonizing. But he was not that kind of man, and if he had been, he would not have discovered America. He must see that the islands he discovered were settled, the gold trade put on a proper footing and the natives converted; he must make contact with the Grand Khan, or some Oriental potentate greater than Guacanagarí. The rights already granted to him, incident to his offices of Admiral and Viceroy, promised (in his eyes) to be far more lucrative than any estate in Spain could possibly be. More than that, he was in good health, full of en-

ergy, in the prime of life (aged forty-one), and he regarded the
work that God had appointed him to do as just begun.

His sense of a divine mission also appears in the curious Greco-
Latin signature he now adopted, and of which no contemporary
explanation exists. In the entail of his property he describes it as
"an X" (by which he probably meant a Greek Chi) "with an S
over it and an M with a Roman A over it and over that an S,
and then a Greek Y" (by which he probably meant a capital
Upsilon) " with an S over it, preserving the relation of the lines
and points." The way he wrote it is as follows:

$$. \; S \; .$$
$$S \; . \; A \; . \; S$$
$$X \; . \; M \; . \; \Upsilon$$
$$:X\rho o \; FERENS$$

Many attempts have been made to solve the riddle. My own belief is that the initial letters stand for *Servus Sum Altissimi Salva-
toris,* Χριστοῦ *Mariae* 'Υιοῦ. Servant am I of the Most High Saviour,
Christ the Son of Mary. The last line is a Greco-Latin form of his
Christian name, emphasizing his rôle as the bearer of Christianity
to lands that never knew Christ. Even on such brief orders or
chits as have survived he signed himself Χρο FERENS.

Columbus was at court for Whitsuntide, Trinity Sunday and
Corpus Christi, but probably the ceremony that interested him
most was the baptism of the six Indians. The King and Queen
and Infante Don Juan graciously consented to act as their god-
parents. The first in rank, kinsman to Guacanagarí, they christened
"Ferdinand of Aragon"; another, "Don Juan of Castile"; while
the clever interpreter was named "Don Diego." Don Juan remained attached to the royal household and died within two
years; the other five returned with the Admiral to the New
World.

While these baptisms expressed the good intentions of the Sovereigns and, to some extent, of Columbus, toward the Indians, it is notorious that in the Indies themselves conversion and Christian treatment never overcame lust until human greed was satisfied. Almost the entire Taino race was exterminated within half a century. It may be said, however, that the Tainos had their revenge on Europeans through the present that they innocently brought to Spain in their bloodstream — *spirochaeta pallida*, the spirillum of syphilis.

The first recorded outbreak of syphilis in Europe was in 1494 among the soldiers of a French army which marched to Naples and back. Bishop Las Casas, who admired Columbus, loved the Indians, and spent a large part of his life in a vain effort to protect them against exploitation, states categorically in his *Apologetica Historia* of around 1530 that the disease was transmitted to the French army by Spanish women who caught it from the Indians brought to Barcelona by Columbus. He adds that, from repeated questioning of the natives of Hispaniola, he was satisfied that the disease was one of long standing in the New World; so long prevalent, indeed, that the natives did not suffer greatly from it. Among Europeans, however, syphilis promptly assumed the most hideous and malignant forms, with many fatalities, just as measles and smallpox affected the Indians when introduced by Europeans.

This subject is very controversial, but it seems to me that Las Casas was correct. The crew of *Niña* on the return voyage cannot have contracted syphilis, for all were healthy and able to work the ship up to the moment of landing. Columbus more than once remarked how amazing it was that all his people stayed in perfect health during the entire passage. Medical authorities assure me that it would have been impossible for a man infected with syphilis to make a tough voyage of two months without becoming very sick indeed. We have no similar record of *Pinta*, but a Spanish surgeon named Ruy Diaz de Isla, in a book printed in 1539, states that besides the Barcelona outbreak which he mentions "a pilot of Palos called Pinzón" was infected and was attended by him. It will be remembered that no less than three Pinzóns shipped in *Pinta*, and that Martín Alonso, the captain, died shortly after her arrival. It seems highly probable that the Indians whom Columbus brought to Barcelona were so briskly entertained there by the women of the town as to infect them with the spirillum, which almost all natives of Hispaniola carried in their bloodstream, and that some of these women either infected Spanish volunteers in the army of Charles VIII, or that they accompanied that army as camp followers.

Although Columbus stayed for several weeks at Barcelona, he was not merely basking in the sunshine of royalty and being entertained by the nobility and higher clergy.[1] In the first place, he was looking after his own interests. Letters patent of the Sovereigns, granting him a coat of arms, gave him the singular privilege of quartering the royal castle of Castile and lion of León with an archipelago of islands and five anchors, the symbol of admiralty. At the same time the rights and privileges granted him conditionally at Granada the previous April were confirmed. He and his heirs "now and forever" were to be styled Admiral of the Ocean Sea and Viceroy and Governor of "the said islands and mainland that you have found and discovered." As Viceroy he

[1] It was at one of these dinners (if it ever happened) that Columbus pulled the famous egg trick. In answer to a diner who said, "Even if you hadn't done it, some Spaniard would have done so soon," Columbus asked the company to balance a hard-boiled egg. Nobody could, but when it came to him, he beat one end flat, and it stood. The moral was — after a trick is done, it looks easy, but give credit to the fellow who thought it up. The story had already done duty in several biographies of other great men before Benzoni told it about Columbus in his *Historia del Mondo Nuovo* (1565), but, as the Italians say, *Se non è vero è bene trovato.*

could appoint and remove all officials in the Indies and have complete civil and criminal jurisdiction over them; as Admiral he would have jurisdiction over all who sailed the ocean west and south of a line from the Azores to the Cape Verdes. Admiralty jurisdiction meant that he or his deputies could handle all disputes among fishermen or merchant mariners in American waters and try all cases of mutiny, piracy, barratry and the like.

Nobody yet had the faintest notion what enormous wealth would pour in on the Columbus family if all these privileges were literally respected. Sovereigns and Discoverer alike presupposed a trading factory on a cluster of islands not far from the coast of China. Yet, even so, Columbus within twenty years would have become one of the richest men in Europe. As it happened, Ferdinand and Isabella, with little respect for vested rights, began to revoke his privileges before he had gained much profit.

Besides his own business, Columbus had work to do for the Sovereigns. His report on the voyage (commonly called the Columbus Letter) was printed in a black-letter, four-page pamphlet at Barcelona either just before or just after he arrived there.[2] A copy reached Rome before April 18, and a Latin translation, dated April 29, appeared there shortly after. The object of this prompt publication was not to spread the news but to obtain confirmation by the Papacy of the lands newly discovered, as the public law of Europe then required, and Columbus was depended on to prove that his discoveries were outside jurisdiction previously granted to the King of Portugal. Pope Alexander VI (Borgia), a Spaniard who owed his election to Ferdinand and Isabella, let them practically "write their own ticket" in a series of papal bulls. The third and most important of these, dated May 4, 1493,

[2] See Appendix for translation.

drew a line of demarcation along the meridian one hundred leagues (318 nautical miles) west of the Azores. All undiscovered lands east of it would belong to Portugal; all west of it, to Spain.

Columbus undoubtedly suggested this line, because he believed that compass variation changed from east to west, and that boisterous winds of Europe gave way to the gentle trades, on or about that meridian of longitude. According to Bishop Las Casas, it was an entomological boundary as well. He observed that seamen and passengers departing from Spain were tortured by lice and fleas until they reached a hundred leagues west of the Azores, when the insects began to disappear, but upon the return passage they emerged from hiding at the same longitude "in great and disturbing numbers." This myth later described insect life as disappearing at the Equator; readers of *Don Quixote* will remember how, in that famous voyage in the enchanted bark, the Knight of the Rueful Countenance bids Sancho Panza search himself for vermin, in order to ascertain whether or not they have passed the Line!

Nevertheless, the line of demarcation set up by the Pope was not enforced. Portugal protested, and as the hostility of John II would have jeopardized their communications with "The Indies," Ferdinand and Isabella in the Treaty of Tordesillas (1494) consented to push the line to the meridian 370 leagues (1175 miles) west of the Cape Verde Islands. From that new division of the world, Portugal derived her title to Brazil and her claim to Newfoundland.

During the three months that Columbus resided at Barcelona, news of his discovery was spreading, chiefly by means of epistles from Italian residents in Spain, and from the printed Letter, the Latin translation of which ran through three editions in Rome in 1493, and about seventeen more, printed in Rome, Paris, Basle and Antwerp, before 1500. But the news traveled very slowly beyond the Alps. The learned men of Nuremberg, center of geographical study in northern Europe, were ignorant of it as late as July 1493, and brother Bartholomew, living near Paris, did not hear of it in time to join the Admiral on his Second Voyage.

Judging from the letters and chronicles, the items in the news that aroused the most attention were gold, naked natives and the opportunity for conversion. Columbus had stressed all three in his printed Letter, as well as the opening of a new trade route to China and the superb scenery and equable climate of the islands he had discovered; but nobody paid any attention to that. Europe was then very short of specie, so that any new gold strike made a universal appeal, as it would today. Fashions in 1493 required women to be heavily clothed from head to foot, so that a community where the natives wore less than a Bikini bathing suit for full dress was news indeed, besides suggesting the state of innocence before Adam's fall. And as Europe had an uneasy conscience at letting Christianity fall back before the Turks, this opportunity to gain souls and redress the balance aroused pleasant anticipations. Of the real significance of the discovery for Europe's future there was not one hint in contemporary comment, nor did anyone venture to suggest that Seneca's prophecy of a vast continent had been fulfilled.

Suppose there had been a popular press on the American model in 1493, Columbus's discovery would have been reported something like this in the leading newspaper of Genoa:

GENOA MAN SEES NAKED NATIVES
FINDS GOLD IN RIVER SANDS
RICH STRIKE FOR KING OF SPAIN

COLOMBO WITH THREE SHIPS REACHES GOLDEN ISLANDS NEAR INDIA
MEN BEAR NO ARMS AND WOMEN WEAR NO CLOTHES

BARCELONA, *March 20.* Our correspondent has heard a strange story of a discovery made for King Ferdinand. Captain Cristóbal Colón, said to be Genoese, reached new islands near India sailing 33 days across Ocean Sea from the Canary Islands, in fleet of 3 caravels. Reports summer climate in winter, natives unlike those of Africa, living in state of nature; men wear nothing but birds' feathers in hair and gold jewelry on arms and legs; women show no shame and wear only small leaf. The Christians were received as gods from Heaven, on an island bigger than all Spain, says Colón, and given all they wanted. The natives have no priests nor lawyers, having neither religion nor laws, and their only weapons are wooden spears, reports the discoverer. Their boats are made of a single tree and carry 70 to 80 men. Rivers in this country are full of gold, asserts the captain, who is now in Seville but is expected shortly to arrive in this city, according to the local Chamber of Commerce. Royal press bureau refused to affirm or deny the report.

Hon. Rafael G. Sanchez, Secretary of the Treasury, when interviewed, said, "This is good news, if true. It will justify public confidence in the administration, and may be considered a victory in our cold war with the Turks." The Rt. Rev. José R. Maggártez, Grand Inquisitor of Spain, released this statement: "This is O.K. provided no subversive Oriental ideas enter Spain. Captain Colón should have cleared with me before bringing Indians home. I shall investigate them on arrival here." Dr. Stephen P. Gomez, well-known professor of geography in the University of Salamanca, when informed, expressed doubt, said he knew Mr. Colón years ago and considered him an impostor. Indies cannot be reached in 33 days, says Prof. Gomez. The Professor is said to have been booed by his students after making this statement. Most people believe the story, and a public reception at City Hall is being planned for Captain Colón when he arrives at Barcelona.

Our reporter, after research in old city directories, identified the discoverer as Cristoforo Colombo, son of Mr. Domenico Colombo of this city. Father Luigi, former teacher of the discoverer, looked up the school records in the presence of our reporter and said he remembered Cristoforo as a good boy, strict in his religious duties, who failed to receive a diploma because he was weak in geography. The father of our distinguished fellow citizen is a retired wool weaver living in the St. John Baptist ward. Contacted at his home, Mr. Colombo was told the news. He said, "It does not surprise me at all.

Chris was always a boy for the girls and the gold. I said he would come to no good, leaving Genoa and going to sea."

Columbus's assertion that he had indeed reached the Indies was accepted at its face value by the Spanish Sovereigns and the Pope, but not by everyone. Peter Martyr d'Anghiera, an Italian humanist at the Spanish court, wrote to a correspondent that the size of the globe seemed to indicate that Columbus could not have reached Asia, and in November 1493 he described the Admiral, in a letter to Cardinal Sforza, as "Novi Orbis Repertor," Discoverer of a New World. Later letters of Peter Martyr indicate that by New World he meant a group of islands which Ptolemy had not described, lying adjacent to the Golden Chersonese (the Malay Peninsula). That is exactly the conclusion reached by Columbus himself in 1498, and by Amerigo Vespucci somewhat later.

CHAPTER X

Second Voyage to America

ALTHOUGH NO VOYAGE, unless it be Magellan's, can ever equal Columbus's First for interest and importance, we must not forget that the Discoverer made three more voyages to America, each of which was sufficient to place him in the first rank of the world's navigators. Of these the Second was most formidable, with the biggest fleet, and in the course of it Columbus discovered the Lesser Antilles, Jamaica and Puerto Rico, explored the south coast of Cuba and effected the first permanent settlement of Europeans in the New World.

The Second Voyage was organized at Cadiz. "You are already at sea, in Cadiz," writes Tomlinson. "You lean your elbows on the rail of a white city afloat in the blue, launched well out into space from the land." The great landlocked gulf is behind you, and off the walls of the town, white as whitecaps on a sunlit sea, there is an open roadstead where vessels can anchor only when the wind is right. The inner harbor behind the breakwater, where we in the Harvard Columbus Expedition moored in 1939, was constructed long after Columbus's day.

While in 1492 it required the utmost persuasiveness to induce any but the very young and adventurous to ship with Columbus, now the Admiral was embarrassd by the number of volunteers. His fame and golden expectations of his discovery were at their zenith. Thousands of men and boys were eager to go out with him and make their fortunes.

The Sovereigns endorsed his proposal to establish a trading-post colony in Hispaniola and gave him practically carte blanche as to means. On May 29, 1493, they issued their instructions. Prime object of the Second Voyage is to be the conversion of the natives, for which purpose six priests are assigned to the fleet, and the Admiral must see to it that the Indians are "treated very well and lovingly." If that were the prime object, it is strange that more and abler priests were not appointed, since the six who did go took three years to win their first convert. In any case, priests were outnumbered at least two hundred to one by lay-men, who were recruited for the second declared objective, the establishment of a trading colony. And, thirdly, the Admiral was charged to explore Cuba and ascertain whether or not it was the Asiatic mainland leading to the golden cities of Cathay.

Every colonizing power in America, down through the seventeenth century, followed this Spanish precedent of loudly and frequently declaring that its first motive was to bring Christianity to the Indians. Whether they really meant it, or were simply making the gesture to obtain divine approval, I leave it to the psychologists to determine. Performance in every instance, except that of the French in Canada, fell woefully short of promise.

Although Columbus was designated "Captain General of the Armada," his friend Don Juan de Fonseca, Archdeacon of Seville, was appointed to organize the fleet while the Admiral completed his diplomatic business at court and fulfilled his vows on the First Voyage. In June, accompanied by the five converted Indians and his younger brother Diego, he set forth from Barcelona. After passing through Madrid and Toledo, he took the pilgrims' road to Guadalupe in the Estremadura, passing through Trujillo, where a thirteen-year-old boy named Francisco Pizarro, the future conqueror of Peru, was then engaged in caring for his father's herd of swine. Columbus prayed long and fervently before the famous Virgin of Guadalupe, and the monks asked him to name an island after her shrine. En route to Seville, he passed through the little town of Medellín, where a small boy named Hernán Cortés must have seen him pass.

Early in July Columbus arrived at Cadiz. Fonseca, according to contemporary standards, had done an excellent job of organizing this, the biggest overseas colonizing expedition ever sent out by a European nation. He had bought or chartered seventeen vessels, victualed them for a round voyage of six months, recruited at least twelve hundred sailors, soldiers and colonists, and collected the necessary seeds, plants, domestic animals, tools and implements for the colony. The Sovereigns ordered all officials of Andalusia to grant Fonseca every facility to purchase provisions at the standard rate. Accounts have been preserved of payments to twenty-five different citizens of Jerez for wheat at 73 maravedis a bushel, about fifteen cents in gold value. Others were paid to grind it into flour and bake ship biscuit — the "hardtack" that formed the staple diet of sailors almost to our own day. Beefs and swine had be rounded up, slaughtered and pickled in brine. Wine had to be purchased by the hogshead and furnished in stout oaken casks that could stand a voyage. Here Columbus had a real complaint: many of the casks were secondhand and let so much wine leak out that Spaniards in Hispaniola endured the incredible hardship of having nothing but water to drink for months! One curious element in the expedition was a cavalry troop of twenty lancers, who sold their fine Arab chargers in Cadiz, purchased some sorry hacks and lived high on the difference; but the substitute nags proved to be good enough to terrorize the natives of Hispaniola.

Of the seventeen vessels of the fleet we know the names of very few. The biggest, named *Santa María* like the flagship on the First Voyage, was a big, brave ship nicknamed *Maríagalante*. Two others that rated as *naos* (ships) were called *Colina* and *La Gal-*

lega. There were about ten square-rigged caravels, of which gallant *Niña* is the only one we can name. And there were at least two lateen-rigged caravels and even smaller Cantabrian barques, which were taken along for shoal-water exploration.

Of the personnel, the Pinzón family were conspicuously absent, but four members of the Niño family of Moguer were on board. Most of the sailors were from around Huelva, as on the First Voyage. No women were taken. Everyone was on the royal payroll except about two hundred gentlemen volunteers.

Unfortunately, no official log or journal of this Second Voyage has survived, but we have good detailed accounts from three participants — Dr. Diego Chanca, the fleet surgeon; Michele de Cuneo of Savona near Genoa, a childhood friend of Columbus; and Melchior Maldonado, a former Spanish diplomat whose account is the basis of Peter Martyr's in his *Decades of the New World.* Columbus, moreover, told Andrés Bernáldez, a Spanish chronicler with whom he stayed at the conclusion of the voyage, many details which Bernáldez set down in his History.

On September 25, 1493, a bright autumn day with a light offshore breeze, "this fleet so united and handsome," as Columbus called it, departed Cadiz. Every vessel flew the royal standard of Castile at her main staff on the high poop, and every skipper dressed ship with the big, brightly colored banners of the day. Waistcloths were stretched between forecastle and poop, and on them were emblazoned the arms of the gentlemen volunteers. A fleet of row-galleys from Venice, which happened to be in the harbor, escorted the ships and caravels to the open sea, with music of trumpets and harps and the firing of cannon.

On October 2 the fleet called at the Grand Canary, and on the fifth at Gomera, where Doña Beatriz de Bobadilla was the lady captain. Columbus had become *tincto d'amore,* literally, "dyed with love," for her on his previous visit, according to his friend

Cuneo. The fact that she now received his fleet with salvos of cannon and fireworks may not mean anything, but if Doña Beatriz expected to play Circe to this Ulysses, she was disappointed. Columbus tarried only a few days, and most of that time was spent in a hasty roundup of more provisions and livestock.

Whether Columbus departed in a hurry because the lady had rejected him, or whether he left a weeping and disconsolate dame behind, or whether love had merely cooled off, we do not know. Doña Beatriz would have been a very proper wife for the now "Very Magnificent Don Cristóbal Colón, Almirante del Mar Océano, Virrey de las Indias." Probably, however, as a practical young widow of much experience, she did not want a sailor for a second husband but a man who would stay at home and look after her and her small boy. Eventually she found him, in the person of the conqueror of the Grand Canary Island, and lived happily ever after.

No two chroniclers agree as to the exact date when the fleet sailed from Gomera, but it ran into the usual Canary calms and took its final departure from Ferro either on the first anniversary of the discovery of America, or on October 13. The Admiral set a course west by south. Although his destination was Navidad, he did not wish to repeat the route of the First Voyage, but to shorten the ocean passage and make discoveries in the Lesser Antilles. It will be remembered that the Indians told him that Matinino (Martinique), the reputed Isle of Women, was the nearest to Spain, and that Charis (Dominica) was next to it on the north side. Now, west by south was the correct rhumb-line course from Gomera to Martinique. How did Columbus figure it out? Actually, as we shall see, he made the next island, the course to which was west and a half south, but that probably happened because his flagship's compass was adjusted to half a point easterly variation.

The ocean passage was uneventful except for a thundersquall on St. Simon's Eve (October 26) which split a number of sails and lighted those ghostly flares which sailors call corposants on the tips of the masts and yards. All the rest of the way the ships enjoyed fair wind and made the 2600 nautical miles from Ferro to Dominica in twenty-one or twenty-two days, an average of 5 knots.

This outward passage must have been very close to a sailor's dream of the good life at sea. Sailing before the trades in a square-rigger is as near heaven as any seaman expects to be on the ocean. You settle down to the pleasant ritual, undisturbed by shifts of wind and changes of weather. There is the constant play of light and color on the bellying square sails (silver in moonlight, black in starlight, cloth-of-gold at sunset, white as the clouds themselves at noon), the gorgeous deep blue of the sea, flecked with whitecaps, the fascination of seeing new stars arise, the silver flash when a school of flying fish springs from the bow wave, the gold and green of leaping dolphins. And on this Second Voyage of Columbus there were seventeen ships in company, so that from the high-pooped flagship one could see white sails all around the horizon. Every day the faster vessels romped ahead, racing one another, but toward sundown, as the hour of singing the *Salve Regina* approached, all closed *Maríagalante*. Imagine the beautiful spectacle, and what good ship handling it required! The Admiral wanted each within hailing distance so that he could give night orders and commendations or reproofs. As night falls, every ship lights her stern lantern or kindles light-wood and oily rags in an iron cresset, and throughout the hours of darkness, during which the trade wind blows full and steady, all try to keep assigned stations, as in a modern convoy. Every half hour the voices of ship's boys announce the turning of the glass; at eleven, at three and at seven o'clock the watch is changed. Just before the morning watch goes on, a priest on board the flagship celebrates what used to be called a "dry Mass" — going through all the motions but not actually consecrating the elements, lest the rolling of the ship cause them to be spilled or dropped. On the other vessels the men watch for the elevation of the host as the signal to kneel and cross themselves; then a hymn is sung, the glass is turned, the watch relieved, and everyone cracks on sail to race the others during the daylight hours.

On All Saints' Day the Admiral was so confident of making land within seventy-two hours that he issued an extra allowance of water. At sundown November 2 he knew land was near, as experienced seamen do, by the gathering of clouds over the horizon ahead and the flight of birds. He ordered sail to be shortened that night, lest they overrun the land in the darkness — there was to be no moonrise until shortly before dawn. An anxious night it must have been, the young men imagining they saw lights and heard breakers, leadsmen heaving the deep-sea lead and singing out, "No bottom," officers testy and irritable. At five in the morning of Sunday, November 3, just as the first faint gray of dawn appeared in the east, a lookout in *Maríagalante* noted ahead a dark cone blotting out a small section of the star-studded horizon. He sang out, *Albricias! Que tenemos tierra!* "The reward! For we have land!" The cry of *Tierra! Tierra!* passes from ship to ship; all is bustle and excitement, and the Admiral summons all hands to prayer on the quarterdeck, where they sing the *Salve* and other hymns, "very devoutly, giving thanks to God for so short and safe a voyage."

CHAPTER XI

Coasting the Caribbees

IT WAS THE BIG, high island of Dominica that they saw, so named by the Admiral from his Sunday landfall, and Dominica it still is. The most amazing thing about this voyage is that Columbus hit the Lesser Antilles at the exact spot recommended by sailing directions for the next four centuries! At that point there is a clear passage between the islands, without dangerous reefs, and once inside the island chain you are almost certain to have a fair wind, whether you are bound for Venezuela and the Spanish Main, or Vera Cruz and the western Caribbean, or the Leeward Islands, Puerto Rico, Santo Domingo and Cuba. The same entrance was used by German submarines in World War II.

As the light increased on November 3 and the fleet sped westward, they picked up next a round, flat island which Columbus named Santa María Galante as a tribute to his flagship, and a group of islands which he called Todos los Santos for the day of All Saints just passed. They are still Mariegalante and Les Saintes. Not yet knowing that there are no harbors on the windward side of the Lesser Antilles, Columbus searched along the ironbound eastern coast of Dominica in vain for an opening, and finally settled on an anchorage on the lee side of Mariegalante. There he went ashore with the banners and took possession for Spain, while the secretary of the fleet recorded everything in proper legal form.

During the day a high island was sighted a few leagues to the westward, and as Mariegalante did not offer anything of value or interest, Columbus ordered anchors aweigh and course set thither. The island he saw was the big, kidney-shaped one which he named Santa María de Guadalupe, as he had promised. Guadeloupe, as the French called it, is now their oldest colony; it became a sugar island so valuable that the British in 1763 seriously thought of swapping it for Canada.

As Columbus's fleet approached Guadeloupe, they saw the strange and beautiful sight of a high waterfall, slender as a silver thread, that appeared to plunge right out of the clouds hanging over the mountains. The vessels anchored under the southern slope of the island's five-thousand-foot volcano, in a sheltered bay now called Grande Anse, and there remained five or six days.

Columbus did not intend to stay more than one night, but his first shore party under Diego Marques got lost in the jungle. That is not surprising, since this was the first lush, dense tropical rain forest that Spaniards had ever encountered. The Admiral did not dare to leave them behind to be picked up later, since there would have been nothing but bones to pick — the natives here were the dreaded man-eating Caribs. Diego's men were finally located by one of four search parties, of fifty men each. In the course of their wanderings, the searching Spaniards learned a good deal about the manners and customs of the Caribs, the race from which the word cannibal is derived. In huts deserted by the natives they found human limbs and choice cuts of human flesh, partly consumed, as well as emasculated boys who were being fattened to provide the *pièce de résistance* for a feast, and girl captives who were used to produce babies for the hors d'oeuvres. Two boys and "twelve very beautiful plump girls from fifteen to sixteen years old" were taken along by the Spaniards. The girls, Tainos who had been captured in a raid on Hispaniola, were useful as interpreters, and doubtless in other ways too.

From Guadeloupe on, the fleet enjoyed a spectacular passage with quartering or beam wind along the leeward coasts of the Lesser Antilles. Those waters afford the finest winter sailing in the world. Each island is a mountain peak rising three, four, or five thousand feet from the Caribbean, whose depths, a few hundred yards from shore, are deepest sapphire blue, while the shoals vary from brilliant emerald to luminous golden yellow. At dawn the next island ahead is a vague shadow, a dark shape against the celestial sphere. With the increase of light, and upon one's own swift approach, the land takes form, substance and color. One can watch the sun kindle the mountain pinnacles to flame, while the forested slopes turn from gray to green, and finally to a blue a few shades lighter than the sea. During the forenoon watch, as the wind makes up, it forms clouds over each island, and if you make the leeward coast by noon, you are apt to be becalmed under the heights; that happened to Columbus at Guadeloupe. Then the sea becomes a gently undulating mirror, reflecting the colors of the land and broken only by flights of flying fish and leaping dolphins. But the calm never lasts long. The wind springs up again, you leave the island astern and gaze back to it, fascinated, as showers lash the forested slopes and the clouds turn orange with the declining sun. And if the western horizon is clear, the sun as it dips below sends up a brilliant emerald flash from its spectrum.

Columbus, even more than most sailors, was devoted to the Virgin Mary, protectress of mariners, and for several days he named almost every island after one or another of her shrines. Some of his names were later transferred to other islands, since it is difficult to keep such a long chain of them straight in one's mind, and the famous chart by Juan de la Cosa, the Admiral's shipmate on this voyage, is confusing. But we can trace the fleet's course with some confidence.

Next after Guadeloupe the fleet passed an island that Columbus named Santa María de Monserrate from a famous monastery near Barcelona; it is still called Montserrat. Next came a tiny round island that has never been settled which he called Santa María la

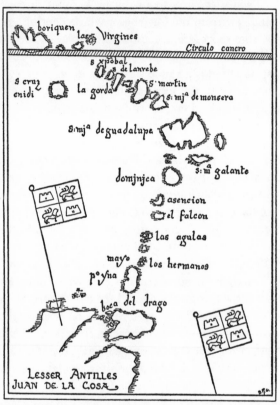

THE CARIBBEE ISLES ON JUAN DE LA COSA'S MAP

Redonda. Several leagues to windward he saw but did not visit a large island which he named Santa María la Antigua, after a famous painting of the Virgin in Seville. During the night of November 11–12, the fleet lay at anchor in the lee of an island which the Admiral named St. Martin, because it was the vigil of the feast of Saint Martin of Tours. This was probably not the present Franco-Dutch island of St. Martin, but Nevis, a name which Columbus apparently gave to Saba. Originally it was "Santa María de la Nieve," St. Mary of the Snow, so called from the pretty story that Santa Maria Maggiore, the second-oldest church in Rome, was built on the Esquiline because the Virgin, in order to indicate her chosen site, caused snow to fall there in August.[1]

Close to Nevis is the present St. Kitts, which Columbus traditionally named after his own patron saint because the shape of the mountain resembled a giant carrying someone pick-a-back. Next comes the island of St. Eustatius, which is possibly a corruption of Columbus's St. Anastasia; seamen call it "Statia" to this day.

The night of November 12–13 was spent by the fleet hove-to off lofty, cone-shaped Saba. What a brave sight! Seventeen vessels under short sail, slowly drifting to leeward, lights from the stern lanterns of the big ships and the iron cressets of the smaller vessels reflected on the water. By morning the fleet would have been well scattered, but at break of day each vessel made sail and scurried to the flagship for orders. The Admiral set a course almost due west, to an island whose direction his Indian guides pointed out and named Ayay.

This island, which the Admiral called Santa Cruz, and for which we now use the French form St. Croix, is the first future United States territory discovered by Columbus. Unlike the heavily forested islands that they had passed, St. Croix was intensively cultivated by its Carib inhabitants, and looked like one great garden as they skirted its northern coast. Missing Christiansted Har-

---

[1] I am indebted to my friend Dr. Leonard Olschki for finally making *S.* [*M*] *de la niebe* out of the inscription on the La Cosa map, which others had deciphered as delanrebe, delanesbon, alaresbon, etc.

bor, owing to the outer barrier of reefs, they anchored off a small estuary now called Salt River Bay. And here the Spaniards had their first fight with natives of America.

At noon November 14, Columbus sent an armed boat with twenty-five men to the head of this harbor, where he saw a small village. The inhabitants fled, but as the boat was returning to the flagship, a Carib dugout suddenly came around the point. The Indians at first were stupefied by the sight of the great ships, but presently recovered their senses, and though they numbered only four men and two women, took up their bows and arrows and let fly, wounding two Spaniards, one mortally. The boat rammed and upset the canoe, but the Caribs swam to a rock where they fought like demons until overcome and taken. One of the men had been shot up so that his intestines hung out, and the Spaniards threw him overboard, but he struck out toward shore, holding his guts in one hand. Recaptured, bound hand and foot and again thrown into the sea, "this resolute barbarian," as Peter Martyr calls him, managed to cast off his bonds and swim. He was then shot through and through with crossbow arrows until he died. A horde of Caribs, so painted as to terrify the Spaniards, ran down to the shore, eager for revenge, but they had no weapons that could reach the ships.

This skirmish at Salt River Bay gave the Spaniards a healthy respect for the Caribs, whom in general they left alone, visiting their islands only with strong armed parties and attempting no settlement for many years. Probably the first Carib in history to be subdued was a "very beautiful girl," one of the canoe party, who was captured by Michele de Cuneo in the fight and presented to him by the Admiral as a slave. "Having taken her into my cabin," wrote Cuneo, "she being naked according to their custom, I conceived a desire to take pleasure." She gave him a severe working-over with her fingernails, he "thrashed her well" with a rope's end, and she raised "unheard-of screams," but "finally we came to an agreement in such manner that I can tell you that she seemed to have been brought up in a school of harlots."

Columbus did not care to tarry at St. Croix, lest the Caribs bring up reinforcements and give real battle. Having already noted the rounded tops of a number of islands over the northern horizon, he decided to investigate them. As the ships approached, more and more islands appeared. The Admiral appropriately named them Las Once Mil Virgines after the eleven thousand seagoing Virgins from Cornwall who, according to legend, were martyred by the Huns at Cologne after a pleasant cruise lasting over a year.

To explore these Virgin Islands the Admiral used the smaller caravels and Cantabrian barques. He sent them through the easterly passage to look at Anegada, after which they squared away down the channel later named after Sir Francis Drake, with high and handsome islands on either hand. The sailors marveled at the dazzling colors of some of the rocks and at the pink coral beaches. In the meantime, *Maríagalante* and the larger vessels sailed in deep water south of the two larger islands, St. John and St. Thomas. On the morning of November 18 the fleet again united west of St. Thomas. That day they raised an island which Columbus named Gratiosa after the noble and pious mother of his friend Alessandro Geraldini, who had entertained him in his days of poverty. Unfortunately, that name, recording filial piety and a deep friendship, has been replaced by Vieques, or Crab Island.

After another night hove-to, the fleet made the south coast of a big island which the natives called Boriquen; the Admiral named it for St. John the Baptist. One of his shipmates on this voyage, Ponce de León, decided that Boriquen would do for him, and early in the next century founded the city of San Juan de Puerto Rico. From that city this island has derived its modern name. All day November 19, Columbus's fleet sailed along the steep southern coast of Puerto Rico and on the morning of the twentieth beat into spacious Boqueron Bay at the southwest end. There the men went fishing, took on fresh water and visited a big Carib village from which all the natives had fled.

From Puerto Rico the fleet crossed the Mona Passage, and at eventide November 22 made landfall on Cape Engaño, Hispaniola, the great island discovered on the First Voyage. An Indian whom Columbus had picked up at Samaná Bay in January recognized it and directed the fleet to his home village. He was set ashore, well provided with trading truck, in the hope that he would mitigate the fears of the suspicious Indians there. Apparently that worked, and a number of Ciguayos visited the ships and traded. And the sailor wounded in the fight at St. Croix, who had since died, was here given Christian burial.

From now on Columbus ranged a coast that he had already discovered. Although eager to make contact with his men at Navidad, he anchored behind Monte Cristi in order to investigate a possible site for settlement. There a shore party got the first hint of what had happened to the Navidad garrison. On the banks of the Rio Yaque del Norte they found two dead and naked bodies, so decomposed as to be unrecognizable; but they were bearded, and Indians do not grow beards.

On the evening of November 27 the fleet anchored outside the pass to Cape Haitien harbor and Caracol Bay; the Admiral, in view of what had happened on Christmas Eve, refused to enter in the dark. Flares were lighted and cannon fired, but there was no answer from shore. Late at night a canoe approached, full of Indians calling for "Almirante." When they recognized Columbus, they presented him with gifts from Guacanagarí and assured him that the Spaniards at Navidad were all right — except that a few had died. A gross understatement! Diego Colón, the

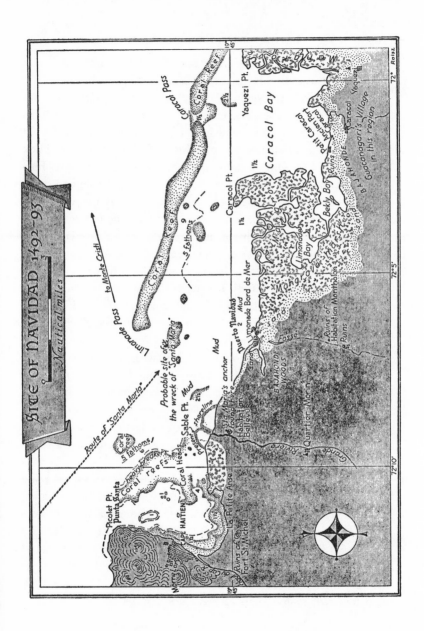

SITE OF NAVIDAD 1492-93

Nautical miles

Route of "Santa Maria"

to Monte Cristi

Limonade Pass

Caracol Pass

Coral Reef

Caracol Reef

Caracol Bay

Yaquezi Pt.

2½

1½

Caracol Pt.

Petit Caracol

BAIE HONDE

Caracol Ancien Port Yaquezi

Caracol Guacanagari's Village in this region

Bekly Bay

Limonade Bay

Mang and Caracol Bay

1½

Puerto Navidad

Limonade Bord de Mer

Mud

2

Ruins of Habitation Montholon

Ruins

St. Ruins

Fosse

Probable site of the wreck of Santa Maria

9 S.Fathoms

Mud

Sta. Maria's anchor

Mud

2½

LIMONADE WOODS

Quartier Morin

Grande Rivière du R. Rivière

Sable Pt.

shoreline

Sta. Maria's grounded place

Habitation Bellevue

Coral Heads

Coral reefs

Heavy breakers

5 Fathoms

Coral reef

Picolet Pt.

Punta Santa

CAPE HAITIEN

Morne

La Petite Anse

Ruins of Fort St. Michel

19°45'

72°

72°5'

72°10'

Reiss.

19°45'

Indian interpreter, got the truth out of them; so horrible a tale that Columbus at first refused to believe it.

The Spaniards at Navidad had acted without reason or restraint. Two of the leaders, including Gutiérrez, the crown official, formed a gang and roamed the island looking for more gold and women than Guacanagarí was able or willing to supply. They fell afoul of Caonabó, cacique of Maguana in the center of Hispaniola, who was made of stouter stuff than the feeble and complacent cacique of Marien. He seized and killed the Gutiérrez gang and then attacked Navidad in order to wipe out the source of trouble. In the meantime, most of the other Spaniards had gone a-roving, so that only ten were left under Columbus's Cordovan friend Diego de Harana to guard the fort. Living with several women apiece, they had posted no guards. Caonabó disposed of them easily, although Guacanagarí did his timid best to prevent him, and then hunted down and slaughtered all the Spaniards who had taken to the bush.

This ended the honeymoon period between Christians and natives. And it reduced the Spaniards' respect for Columbus, who had always dwelt on the timidity of the Tainos and their lack of warlike weapons. Fray Buil, head of the priestly contingent, recommended that Guacanagarí be put to death as an example to the rest; the Admiral refused, and that cacique remained a faithful ally to the Spaniards.

The immediate problem before Columbus was to chose a site for his trading-post colony. Dr. Chanca, the fleet surgeon, ruled out the swampy shores of Caracol Bay, where the natives were friendly, and Cape Haitien seemed too far from the gold-bearing Cibao. So the Admiral decided to sail eastward again in search of a good harbor. Going against the trades and the westward-flowing current meant a long, tedious beat to windward; it took the fleet twenty-five days to make good about thirty-two miles.

Frequent shifting of sail and constant wetting with salt spray wore the sailors down, exasperated the colonists, and killed a large proportion of the livestock. Thus it was that on January 2, 1494, when the fleet anchored in the lee of a peninsula that afforded shelter from the east wind, Columbus decided to pitch his city then and there. It was a settlement founded under an evil star, although named Isabela after the Queen.

Here for the time being discovery ended, as happiness had already ended for Columbus when he learned the fate of Navidad. Yet he must have derived great satisfaction from this voyage to Hispaniola. He had conducted across the Atlantic seventeen vessels, many of them very small, made a perfect landfall, and continued through a chain of uncharted islands, with no accident serious enough to be recorded. He had discovered twenty large islands and over two score small ones upon which the eyes of no European had ever rested. Over the biggest fleet that had yet crossed deep water, bearing twelve hundred seamen, colonists and men-at-arms, he had kept discipline during a voyage that lasted fourteen weeks. In a region inhabited by fierce man-eating Caribs he had avoided conflict save for one brief skirmish, and lost but a single man. Plenty of trouble was awaiting the Admiral when he left the deck of *Maríagalante* for dry land and exchanged the function of Captain General for that of Viceroy. The turn in his fortunes was sharp, and it came quickly. In the years to come, when suffering in body from arthritis and in mind from the ingratitude of princes, Columbus must have sought consolation in the memory of those bright November days of 1493, the fleet gaily coasting along the lofty, verdure-clad Antilles with trade-wind clouds piling up over the summits and rainbows bridging their deep-cleft valleys, of nights spent hove-to with his gallant ships all about, stars of incredible brightness overhead, and hearty voices joining in the evening hymn to the Blessed Virgin.

CHAPTER XII

The First Colony

COLUMBUS, who was already familiar with the trading-post type of colony through his voyages to the Genoese factory at Chios and the Portuguese factory of São Jorge da Mina in Africa, planned to found just such a colony in Hispaniola, for he believed that he would be dealing with a wealthy Oriental race who had vast stores of precious metals, gems and spices which they would be glad to exchange for European wares. The conception was sound, or would have been if the premise had been correct, as the Portuguese and Spaniards later proved through their establishments at Goa in India, Macao in China, and Manila in the Philippines.

Unfortunately for Columbus, the premise was not correct. He had noted with some discomfiture on his First Voyage that the "Indians" had little to sell and even fewer wants, but they kept baiting him with tales of abundant gold in the Cibao, and anyway, was not golden Cathay just around the corner?

So, Isabela was founded as a trading post. Even as such it was ill chosen. Almost all the first European colonies in America were pitched on impossible sites — for instance, Roanoke Island and Dochet Island on the St. Croix River. Isabela was no exception. There was no fresh water handy and no proper harbor, only a roadstead open to the north and west. The place was swarming with malaria-carrying mosquitoes. But Columbus was in a hurry to get his men ashore and send the ships home. He had wasted a month looking for a site which the Navidad garrison should have found, and the barrel of gold nuggets which they should have collected was not there. He must start trading quickly and produce something valuable to please his Sovereigns.

So all the colonists and some of the seamen were landed at Isabela. A town was laid out in classic form (for nothing less than a miniature Cadiz would suit the Admiral), with church and governor's palace fronting on a square plaza. Men were set to work felling trees, cutting coral stone and digging a canal to bring water from the nearest river, and about two hundred wattled huts were built as temporary housing. But insufficient wine and provisions had been brought over. Workers fell ill of malaria or from drinking well water and eating strange fish, although Dr. Chanca tried every new species on a dog before he would let any Christian touch it. Columbus, impatient to get things done, drafted some of the gentlemen volunteers for the hard labor, which caused great indignation; they had come out to fight or get gold, not to do menial work. If they refused, they got no rations, and that was considered an abominable way to treat a Castilian hidalgo.

Many, however, were appeased by an early opportunity to gather gold. Isabela had been founded only four days when the Admiral organized an armed party to explore the Cibao and find the alleged mine. It was commanded by Alonso de Hojeda, an agile, wiry and handsome Andalusian who had attracted the Queen's notice and obtained command of a caravel by the singular feat of pirouetting on a beam that projected from a tower two hundred feet above a street in Seville.

Hojeda, with a score or more of Spaniards and a number of native guides, penetrated the great central valley of Hispaniola and reached the foothills of the Cordillera Central in the Cibao. There he found plenty of evidence of gold and obtained three great nuggets, one with metal enough for a fifty-dollar gold piece. Within two weeks, on January 20, he was at Isabela, bringing the first good news for many weeks. "All of us made merry," wrote Cuneo, "not caring any longer about spicery, but only for this blessed gold."

The Admiral feared that if he sent the ships home with nothing more than what Hojeda brought in, the King might make sneering remarks about Columbus's line of samples. Yet he had to risk it, since the crews of seventeen ships were accumulating pay and using up food, several hundred men were sick, Dr. Chanca was out of drugs, and there were barely enough Spanish provisions left to get the fleet home. So, retaining only *María-galante, Gallega, Niña* and two smaller caravels, he dispatched the other twelve vessels under command of his flag captain, Antonio de Torres. The cargo they carried, though jeered at by royal officials as "so-called cinnamon, only it tasted like bad ginger; strong pepper, but not with the flavor of Malayan pepper; wood said to be sandalwood, only it wasn't"; sixty parrots and twenty-six Indians, actually was topped off with gold to the value of 30,000 ducats — roughly equivalent to 14,000 sovereigns or 3500 double eagles. A pretty good sample, indeed!

Torres made a quick homeward passage, arriving at Cadiz on March 7, only twenty-five days after leaving Hispaniola. As brother to the governess of the Infante Don Juan, Torres had access to the Sovereigns and so was entrusted by Columbus with the outlines of a report to present to them orally. This "Torres Memorandum," as it is called, is intensely interesting both as the result of the Admiral's first four weeks' colonial experience and for the comments on it by Ferdinand and Isabella.

Columbus trusts Torres to tell the Sovereigns all about the gold, especially about the manner in which it is panned out from river sand. He excuses himself for not sending more because many of

his men have fallen sick, a strong garrison has to be kept at Isabela, and with no beasts of burden to carry the heavy metal the
accumulation of a shipload would require too much time. Ferdinand and Isabella gave this the royal O.K., with "great thanks
to God" for the discovery of the gold.

Next, the Admiral enjoins Torres to tell their Highnesses that
the cause of the prevalent sickness "is the change of water and
air; . . . the preservation of health depends upon this people being provided with the food to which they are accustomed in
Spain." As it will take time for the wheat and barley that he has
planted to make a crop, and for the vines and rattoons that he
has set out to bear grapes and sugar cane, food must be supplied
from Spain, particularly wine, ship biscuit, bacon and pickled
beef. Few livestock have survived the voyage, so he also needs
cattle and sheep, and asses and mares to breed mules. He would
also appreciate a few luxuries for the sick, such as sugar, raisins,
rice, almonds and honey. Clothing was another problem. In that
hot, rough country the Spaniards were rapidly wearing out
clothes and shoes; Columbus wants quantities of each, as well
as cloth and leather, to be sent out and sold at reasonable prices.
And he needs a hundred more firearms, a hundred crossbows, two
hundred cuirasses for protection against poisoned arrows, and
plenty of powder and lead.

Logistic supply was a major problem for all European pioneers; it will be remembered how the first English settlers in
Virginia rotted and starved for want of their native bread, beef
and beer in a country abounding with maize, game and good
water, and how the Pilgrim Fathers were constantly running
into debt for consignments of clothing and shoes, which they
had no means of making for themselves.

Ferdinand and Isabella felt that their Viceroy's requests were
reasonable. They ordered Archdeacon Fonseca, organizer of the

fleet, to make prompt arrangements to send out more seeds, roots and cattle, and to provide all the other items that the Admiral wanted, except that they did not view favorably his suggestion of an official clothing and shoe store.

Columbus says that he is sending home some of the "canibales" captured at St. Croix, in order that they may be converted, weaned from their beastly appetites, and learn Castilian so that they can be used as interpreters. He then develops the idea (already mentioned in his Letter on the First Voyage) that Carib or other Indian slaves might be very profitable to export from Hispaniola, and that men might be employed to raid the Caribbee Islands with that object in view. Slavery was so taken for granted in those days, both by Europeans and by the Moslems (who still practice it), that Columbus never gave a thought to the morality of this proposal. If he had, he would doubtless have reflected that the Indians enslaved each other, so why should we not enslave them, particularly if we convert them, too, and save their souls alive? The Sovereigns did not welcome the slave-trade proposal and replied that they would reserve judgment on it until they could learn more details. Isabella eventually forbade it, but not until it had proved to be unprofitable.

The Admiral concluded his memorandum by a generous tribute to Dr. Chanca and other subordinates, asked to have their salaries raised, and recommended that the two hundred gentlemen volunteers be placed on the royal payroll so that they could be controlled.

Most of this memorandum shows sound common sense on the part of the Discoverer, and a flexibility that was not usual with him. His trading-post idea is evidently going down the drain, simply because the Indians of Hispaniola were not traders, and, after their curiosity was satisfied, cared little or nothing for European goods. It is no longer a factory that he wants, but a beachhead — a springboard to conquest. Almost as an "aside," Columbus proposed that the Sovereigns send him a delegation of miners from the quicksilver mines of Estremadura. He had already observed that to obtain gold in any quantity the Spaniards must go out and get it, a procedure which turned out to be very unfortunate for the Indians.

About a month after sending the fleet home under Torres, Columbus organized and in person led a reconnaissance in force of the interior, first of those overland marches of Spaniards in armor which set the pattern followed by Balboa, Cortés, Pizarro and Coronado. In military formation with drums beating, trumpets sounding and banners displayed, several hundred men started south from Isabela on March 12, 1494. Crossing the Cordillera Setentrional by a pass which Columbus named El Puerto de los Hidalgos after his gentlemen trailmakers, they soon came in view of a spacious valley "so fresh, so green, so open, of such color and altogether so full of beauty," wrote Las Casas, that "the Admiral, who was profoundly moved by all these things, gave great thanks to God and named it Vega Real," the Royal Plain. The hidalgos marched between maize fields, under mahogany, ebony and silk-cotton trees, and past villages where they were offered little packets of gold dust. Crossing the Rio Yaque del Norte by canoe or raft, or on the backs of friendly Indians, they pushed up the northern slope of the Cordillera Central to a mesa overlooking a bend of the Rio Janico, where Columbus left fifty men to construct a rough earthen fort. One of his ablest lieutenants, Pedro Margarit, was left in command of this fort, which was named Santo Tomás as a joke on one of the hidalgos who doubted the existence of gold in Hispaniola. While some stayed there, others climbed the mountains to prospect for gold and collected a fair quantity. "On that trip," wrote Cuneo, "we spent twenty-nine days with terrible weather, bad food and worse drink; nevertheless, out of covetousness for that gold, we all kept strong and lusty."

Those left behind at Isabela were neither strong nor lusty. They had found no gold to compensate for living and working in that unhealthy spot, and almost the last of the Spanish provisions were spent. Discontent was rife, mutiny was seething, several troublemakers were in irons, and as a precaution Columbus placed all arms and munitions on board his flagship with brother Diego in command.

To raise morale and get rid of the troublemakers, he now planned a second reconnaissance in force under Hojeda, consisting of four hundred men with orders to march to Santo Tomás, relieve Margarit's garrison, which was in danger of attack, and then explore the country and live off the natives. This was one of Columbus's worst decisions. He instructed Hojeda to do the Indians no harm and reminded him that the Sovereigns desired their salvation even more than their gold, but the first thing that Hojeda did was to cut off the ears of an Indian who stole some old Spanish clothes. Next, he manacled the cacique whom he considered responsible and sent him in chains to Isabela. Hojeda then relieved Margarit, who, with three hundred and fifty to four hundred Spaniards, roamed the Vega Real extorting gold from the natives, exhausting their food supplies, carrying off boys as slaves and young girls as concubines.

Before there was time for Columbus to learn of these doings, he had departed to explore Cuba, leaving his younger brother in charge at Isabela. Las Casas describes Diego as "a virtuous person, very discreet, peaceable and simple," who really wanted to be a bishop. He was incapable of raising the morale of the colonists, much less of controlling egoists like Hojeda and Margarit. But Columbus felt that there was no one else in all the colony whom he could trust.

CHAPTER XIII

Exploring Cuba

WHEN COLUMBUS once adopted a geographical theory, it was almost impossible for him to give it up. He had now explored enough of Hispaniola to decide that it bore no resemblance to the Japan described by Marco Polo. Yet, if Cibao were not Cipangu, might it not be Sheba, the kingdom of Ophir, whence came a famous Queen with gifts for King Solomon? Anyway, was not Cuba a promontory of Asia? That was one of the things which the Sovereigns had ordered him to investigate. In the famous Letter on the First Voyage, he refers to Cuba both as an island and as a province of Cathay, but, between voyages, he had in his own mind decided that Cuba was the Chinese Province of Mangi. That was the name which Marco Polo gave to all South China.

So, having dispatched Hojeda to the Cibao, the Admiral resumed his congenial rôle of discoverer. *Niña*, the tried and true, again served as flagship; the other two vessels of the Cuban fleet were lateen-rigged *San Juan* and *Cardera*. They are described as "much smaller" than *Niña* and carried crews of only 14 to 16 as compared with her 28 to 30. So, as *Niña* measured 55 to 60 tons and was not over 70 feet long, these small caravels must have measured less than 40 tons and could hardly have exceeded 50 feet in length. For officers, Columbus had one of the loyal Niños and Pedro de Terreros and several other veterans of his First Voyage. Fortunately for history, Columbus's gossipy friend

Michele de Cuneo shipped as passenger, and Juan de la Cosa the chartmaker as able seaman. "Diego Colón," the best of the Taino converts, came along as interpreter, and there was one priest, whose name is not known.

The three caravels sailed from Isabela April 24, 1494. It was the best season for navigating the Greater Antilles, when the trades can be depended on by day and there is an offshore breeze at night; the air is still cool, and there is no danger of a hurricane. On the twenty-ninth they crossed the Windward Passage to Cape Alpha and Omega, as Columbus had named Cape Maisi on his First Voyage. There he landed, set up a column and a cross and again took formal possession of Cuba for Spain. On the advice of his officers, the Admiral decided to range the south rather than the north coast, "because should there be anything good it would rather be to the southward than the northward." This was Aristotle's ancient theory, supported by Portuguese experience in Africa, that the farther south one sailed, the more gold and precious wares would be encountered.

From Cape Maisi on, the Spaniards made fresh discoveries. They sailed West by South for fifty miles along a cliff-rimmed coast, noting (as we modern mariners did in our ketch *Mary Otis*, about the size of *Cardera*) the sweet scent of the land — a combination of sea grape, cactus flowers and various aromatic plants. As evening fell on the last day of April, they entered a great sickle-shaped harbor which Columbus named Puerto Grande. This was Guantanamo Bay, seat of an important United States naval base in the twentieth century. A shore party found that the natives had fled in the midst of cooking a gigantic dinner of fish, iguana and hutia (the small Cuban quadruped) for their own chief, who was about to entertain a visiting cacique. The cooks were persuaded by "Diego Colón" to return and share the feast with the Spaniards. They were well paid with hawks' bells and other trifles for their trouble of catching more fish to regale the cacique, but were relieved that their uninvited guests refused to touch iguana meat, since roast iguana was the favorite native delicacy. The Spaniards remarked that they would as soon eat an alligator.

On May Day morning the fleet departed with the land breeze. The Guantanamo Indians had passed the word by "grapevine," so, as the ships sailed close to the bold shore, multitudes flocked to the water's edge or paddled out in canoes, offering cassava bread and sweet water and begging the "men from the sky" to call. It will be remembered that there had been no unfortunate incidents between Spaniards and natives in Cuba; race relations there were still of the "Golden Age," and Columbus, to his credit, so kept them to the end of this voyage.

Forty miles west of Guantanamo the Admiral noted a break in the sierra and sailed through a cliff-bordered channel only 180 yards wide into the great bay where, twenty years later, Velasquez founded the city of Santiago de Cuba. Again, relations with the natives, who had "the loveliest gardens in the world," were idyllic. Departing at dawn May 2, the fleet sailed through the waters in which the Battle of Santiago was fought four centuries later, as a result of which Cuba ceased to be a Spanish colony.

After a very fast run, Columbus landed at a cape that he named Cabo de Cruz (as it is still called) because it was the accepted date of the discovery of the True Cross. Here, instead of turning into the Gulf of Guacanayabo, the Admiral decided to take off for Jamaica, the existence of which he had been told by the Indians at Santiago. Its native name — Jamesque — sounded so like the golden isle of Babeque, about which he had been told on the First Voyage, that he hoped here to find gold; for in Cuba, so far as he could ascertain, there was none.

The trades blew up strong and the fleet had a rough passage

of two days, part of the time hove-to. Since it had been "all hands on deck" for many hours, Columbus gave Alonso Medel, master of *Niña*, permission to send all hands below for a much needed rest as soon as she was hove-to. Later the Admiral, noting that the weather was moderating, came on deck and set about making sail by himself, in order not to disturb the weary watch. I do not imagine he could have done much more than cast off the gaskets from the mizzen and trim the braces of the small fore-yard before others were awakened by the slatting of sails and the change of motion. But the incident illustrates the consideration that Columbus showed to his people, and helps to explain the loyalty of his sailors, despite the many hardships he led them into and the few rewards that his voyages brought them.

On May 5 the fleet anchored in St. Ann's Bay, Jamaica, which Columbus named Santa Gloria. He declared that this island was "the fairest that eyes have beheld" and the most heavily populated of the Greater Antilles. Sixty or seventy Indian warriors in big dugout canoes came out to meet the fleet and showed every intention to fight, but a cannon shot sent them back to shore. Since Columbus wanted wood and water, as well as a chance to calk one of the caravels, he proceeded to the next port west, Rio Bueno. There the Indians put on another hostile demonstration, but Columbus sent the ships' boats away, armed with crossbowmen who "pricked them well and killed a number." When they were ashore, he set upon them a great dog which bit some Indians severely and chased off the rest. These tactics of worrying Indians with savage dogs were currently being practiced in Hispaniola, as they earlier had been on the Guanches in the Canaries. The natives of Rio Bueno, who also were Tainos, promptly appeased the Spaniards with provisions, but they were unable to produce gold. So the Admiral made one more call in Jamaica, at Montego Bay, then sailed back on the starboard tack to Cape Cruz.

The fleet now resumed its exploration of the south Cuban coast, alert for evidences of Chinese culture. They sailed around the Gulf of Guacanayabo and at sunrise May 15 sighted an archipelago of small islands. These were the group inshore of the Laberinto de Doze Leguas; Columbus named the archipelago El Jardin de la Reina, the Queen's Garden.[1] According to his description, these cays were then very beautiful; some were cultivated by the natives, and others were adorned with royal palms and calabash trees. The Spaniards admired "great birds like cranes, but bright red" — flamingoes — and watched the natives hunting turtle with tame fish. An Indian would catch young and train a pilot fish with suckers on his head and let it out on a leash when turtles were about. The fish would attach himself to a turtle, and the Indian only had to haul it in. This was one of Columbus's tales that Europeans found most difficult to believe, but it was true; and Cubans still practice the same method of catching turtle.

We in 1940 found the "Queen's Garden" a sad disappointment. Mangrove has driven all other plants off these cays, and most of the mangrove is dead. But the channels between them are so intricate and shallow that we felt Columbus must have been as good a navigator in shoal water as he was on the ocean.

The three caravels put to sea through the Boca Grande, then shaped a course for the Sierra de Trinidad. As they sailed along the bold coast of this sierra, natives again flocked to the shore bearing gifts and welcoming the Spaniards as "men from the sky." But, by San Fernando, not one Chinese junk or sampan or tem-

[1] His "Garden" included the Leviza, Cuatro Reales, Manuel Gomez and other cays and the Buena Esperanza bank.

ple or bridge! Could it be that the culture of Cathay had not
reached this outlying part of the Grand Khan's dominions? Or
was this only one more big island?

Columbus missed the narrow entrance to the bay where Cien-
fuegos was later built, but investigated the Gulf of Cochinos,
noting the subterranean streams that break out from under the
sea and enable sailors to fill their water casks without going
ashore. "The water was so cold, and of such goodness and so
sweet," said Columbus, "that no better could be found in the
world." He and a shore party "rested there on the grass by
those springs amid the scent of the flowers, which was marvelous,
and the sweetness of the singing of little birds, so many and so
delightful, and under the shade of those palms, so tall and fair
that it was a wonder to see it all." Andrés Bernáldez set all this
down from the Admiral's own lips. We hardly need labor the
point that Columbus's appreciation of the beauties of nature was
equal to that of eighteenth-century romantics and unique among
pioneers in the age of discovery.

The little fleet now entered the Gulf of Batabanó, where the
Admiral saw a phenomenon that has intrigued many later navigators — water turning as white as milk, and then black as ink.
The white is caused by fine marl becoming roiled by waves in
the shallow sea, and the inky color by black sand similarly
stirred up. The shores of this gulf, said the Admiral in very vivid
language, were of mangrove, "so thick a cat couldn't get ashore."
By May 27 he reached the tip end of the Zapata Peninsula,
which he called Punta del Serafín because it was the feast of
All Angels; he crossed the Ensenada Broa and anchored near the
present town of Batabanó.

And no sign of China! The natives near Trinidad, either to
please the Admiral or because they knew no better, said that the
coast continued westward indefinitely, and that the western re-

gion was called Magón, which Columbus interpreted as the Province of Mangi. And near Batabanó a crossbowman who had been hunting in the forest declared that he had encountered light-complexioned natives wearing white tunics which reached to their knees. Columbus jumped to the conclusion that these were Christians, that he must have skipped China and reached Ethiopia! But that notion did not last long.

Sailing westward along the southern shore of the Province of Pinar del Rio, the caravels became involved in the worst shoals yet experienced. They could get through some channels only by the laborious process of kedging — rowing an anchor ahead, dropping it and hauling the vessel up to it by the windlass while her keel scraped the mud. They even passed the limit of Taino culture and entered the last stronghold of the Siboney, whom "Diego Colón" could not understand.

Captain Lecky remarks in the preface to his famous *"Wrinkles" in Practical Navigation,* "Comparatively few sailors are good mathematicians, and it is fortunate that such is the case; for Nature rarely combines the mathematical talent of a Cambridge wrangler with that practical tact, observation of outward things, and readiness in an emergency, so essential to a successful sea captain." How well that description fits Columbus! He now figured out by mathematics that he was at least half the way around the world, when he was actually less than one quarter — in longitude 84 degrees West of Greenwich. Assuming the Bahía Cortés, where Cuban land trends south, to be the Gulf of Siam, he believed that he needed only to round the Malay Peninsula (Ptolemy's Golden Chersonese) to enter the Strait of Malacca. So, why not return to Spain around the world, hooking up with the tracks of Bartholomew Dias and Vasco da Gama?

Fortunately, the common sense of a good seaman came to the rescue. The caravels were leaky because of frequent groundings;

their rigging was fast becoming shreds and tatters; provisions were low, and the seamen were growling and grumbling. So the Admiral decided to reverse course. Following the precedent established by Dias in 1488 when forced to turn back from the very gates of India, Columbus took a deposition from almost every man in his little fleet to the effect that Cuba must be part of a continent, that it was useless to sail any farther to prove it since no island of that length could exist! Actually, they were then about fifty miles from the western promontory of Cuba. This procedure did not convince even Juan de la Cosa, who represents an insular Cuba on his famous map. For many years European cartographers depicted two Cubas — the true island and a continental one resembling Marco Polo's conception of Mangi, which Columbus insisted was correct.

The return to Isabela began on June 13, 1494. For the most part it was a very tiresome beat to windward among the same cays as on the outward passage, because Columbus could make no progress in deep water against the trade winds and the westward-flowing current. "If the ships in the Indies only sail with the wind abaft the beam," he wrote, "it is not from bad design or clumsiness; the great currents, which run there in the same direction of the wind, so make it that nobody attempts to struggle close-hauled, for in one day they would lose what they gained in seven; nor do I except caravels, even Portuguese lateeners." His good windward record with *Niña* and *Pinta* in 1493 had been made in deep waters where there was no current. Sailing vessels never could cope with the conditions Columbus describes until the advent of the modern racing yacht, and even they usually cope with them by "turning on the juice." William Hickey, writing at St. Mary's, Jamaica, in the last years of the eighteenth century, tells of watching a ship try to beat from Kingston to Port Morant, a distance of only nine or ten miles. Every day she stood out to sea close-hauled on the port tack, and every evening, sailing close-hauled on the starboard tack, she came to the same position offshore. This went on for "eight successive days without her gaining a single mile."

Columbus in 1494 learned that the only way to make progress windward was to stay in smooth water, avoiding the current, and to work the land breeze at night. It took him twenty-five days to make good about two hundred miles. By the time he reached the Queen's Garden he could stand no more mud navigation and steered outside the Laberinto de Doze Leguas into blue water. And it then took him ten days to make one hundred eighty miles to windward. Provisions had to be rationed to a pound of weevily biscuit and a pint of sour wine a day, and the sailors pumped constantly. Finally, on July 18, they reached Cape Cruz and were well entertained by friendly Indians. Rather than endure another long beat to windward along the ironbound coast of Oriente Province, the Admiral decided to ease off his sheets and learn more about Jamaica.

Montego Bay was again entered on July 21. From that future scene of fashion he hauled around the western end of Jamaica to the south coast and edged along, anchoring every night. The Indians were friendly, one cacique embarrassingly so. He came out to the flagship with a fleet of canoes, his family and suite dressed in magnificent parrot-feather headdresses and little else. The cacique wore a coronet of small polished stones and some large disks of gold and copper alloy that he must have obtained from Central America. In the bow of his canoe stood a herald wearing a cloak of red feathers and carrying a white banner. His wife was similarly adorned with native jewelry, although she wore nothing that could be called clothing except "a little cotton thing no bigger than an orange peel"; their daughters, aged about fifteen and eighteen, were completely naked and very beautiful. When this array of savage magnificence drew alongside, the Admiral was so absorbed in reading the office of tierce in his cabin that he did not know what was up until they were all on board. The cacique then proposed, through "Diego Colón," that he and his family sail to Spain with the Admiral to visit the Catholic Sovereigns "and to see the wonders of Castile." Here was a golden opportunity for Columbus to make a hit at court, but humanity prevailed. He thought of the cold weather on the voyage home, of the indignities that the pretty daughters might suffer from the sailors, and of the effect of a complete change of life on these innocent souls. So he sent them ashore with gifts, after receiving the cacique's homage and fealty to Ferdinand and Isabella.

On August 19 the fleet cleared Morant Point, the eastern cape of Jamaica, crossed the Windward Passage and sighted Cape Tiburon, Haiti. By the end of the month they reached Alta Vela, the sail-like rock which marks the southernmost point of Hispaniola. Swarms of Indians paddled out and told him that all was well at Isabela, which was far from correct. Near the site of Santo Domingo he landed a party of nine men and sent them across the island to announce his coming.

Saona Island, behind which the three caravels anchored to ride out a hurricane, was so named for the home town of Michele de Cuneo, the Admiral's merry guest. A total eclipse of the moon took place on September 14 while the fleet was anchored there, and Columbus, who had an almanac which gave the time of the eclipse at Nuremberg, tried by timing it at Saona to calculate the longitude. It is a simple enough calculation — fifteen degrees to an hour's time — but something went wrong. The Admiral worked out his longitude as the equivalent of 91 degrees 30 minutes West of Greenwich, which was 23 degrees too far west — the Pacific coast of Guatemala. Building on that gross error, it was easy for Columbus to persuade himself that he had been well on his way around the world when he turned back from Cuba.

The Admiral intended to make a side trip to Puerto Rico, but while crossing the Mona Passage he became very ill. His symptoms suggest a nervous breakdown as the result of lack of sleep, frequent drenching and inadequate food. Probably he also had the beginnings of arthritis, which troubled him gravely during the last ten years of his life. His officers held a council and decided to scud before the wind to Isabela, where the three caravels anchored on September 29, 1494. The Admiral was carried ashore in the arms of his seamen.

Although Columbus had not found the empire of the Grand Khan, he had accomplished a great deal on this round voyage of five months from Isabela. He had opened up what proved to be the most valuable of Spain's insular possessions and discovered Jamaica, brightest jewel of the old English Empire. He had demonstrated that he was no less apt at coastal piloting and island hopping than at charting a course across the ocean and conducting a fleet in blue water. Shipmates of that voyage never tired of extolling his feats of navigation, his consideration for them and his magnanimity toward the natives.

CHAPTER XIV

Hell in Hispaniola

THE FIRST NEWS that the Admiral received upon landing at Isabela was good. His brother Bartholomew, whom he had not seen for six years, had arrived. Christopher's letter to him in France about the success of the First Voyage had never been delivered, and he reached Spain too late to start with his brother on the Second Voyage. But Ferdinand and Isabella were highly impressed by "Don Bartolomé," as they called him, and gave him command of three caravels to take provisions to Hispaniola, as Columbus had requested.

Christopher was overjoyed to see his brother, who had been his partner in promoting the Great Enterprise and who, in character, was his complement. Bartholomew was not only an expert cartographer but a man of action, a perfect executive to carry out the ideas of his brilliant brother. Intelligent without being an intellectual, he was a good linguist and had an innate sense of leadership. Curt in speech and tough with subordinates, he lacked the "sweetness and benignity" that Las Casas saw in Christopher, but above all he was dependable. He never lost courage or fell ill; he met unexpected situations on land or sea with promptness and resolution.

It is most regrettable that Bartholomew "missed the boat" on the Second Voyage because he, if anyone, could have averted the appalling situation in Hispaniola which the weak younger brother Diego had allowed to develop. It must be said, however, that the three Columbus brothers had two strikes against them from the start, because they were Genoese and the colonists were Spaniards. At that time — and perhaps still — Spain was the most fiercely nationalistic of European nations, and the Spaniards who went to America to seek their fortunes were not only rugged individualists but greedy and unreasonable. Oviedo, in his *History of the Indies* that came out in 1535, wrote that any early governor of Hispaniola, "to succeed, must be superhuman." And Christopher had already made two bad mistakes — appointing Diego his deputy, and turning Hojeda and Margarit loose in the interior.

During the Admiral's absence, Diego heard about the cruelty and rapacity of Margarit and sent him an order to mend his ways, which so enraged the Spaniard that he roared into Isabela demanding retraction — or else. When he didn't get it, he joined other malcontents, who seized the three caravels that Bartholomew Columbus had brought out from Spain, and sailed home. One of those rebel leaders was Fray Buil, the ecclesiastic in charge of conversion. He had not won a single convert among the docile Tainos around Isabela, but had consistently opposed all that the Columbus brothers did. When the stolen caravels arrived in Spain late in 1494, Fray Buil went directly to court to circulate slanders against the Admiral and his brothers, while a Sevillian goldsmith of the party declared openly that none of the gold in Hispaniola was genuine. That probably was a "cover story" for the rebels, who secretly sold their loot without paying the Crown's twenty per cent or the Admiral's ten.

Within a month or two of Columbus's return to Isabela, Antonio de Torres sailed into the roadstead in command of four caravels bringing more provisions and supplies. He delivered a friendly letter to the Admiral from the King and Queen, who urged him to leave Hispaniola in charge of his "brother or some other person" and come home to help them in negotiations with Portugal. Here was an opportunity for Columbus to refute the slanders of Buil and Margarit. But he stayed on, either because he was too ill to face the ocean voyage, or because he wished to get the local situation well in hand. Moreover, in order to provide a profitable export to Spain, since the amount of gold collected for the crown was still short of expectations, he adopted the questionable policy of rounding up and enslaving Indians who had resisted Margarit's men. Time and again Columbus had asserted that the Tainos were the most kindly, peaceful and generous people in the world, and the Sovereigns had particularly enjoined him to treat them as such. But if they resented the very contrary treatment meted out to them, they were faced by the alternatives of slavery or death.

By the close of February, 1495, when Torres was ready to sail to Spain, the Columbus brothers had collected fifteen hundred Indian captives at Isabela. Torres loaded five hundred of them, all his four ships could take. The Admiral then allowed every Spaniard at Isabela to help himself to as many of the remainder as he chose, and the rest were told to get out. Cuneo records how these wretched captives, when released, fled as far as they could from the Spaniards; women even abandoned infants in their fear and desperation to escape further cruelty. At least they were free; the lot of the slaves shipped home was worse. About two hundred died on the voyage, and half the survivors were sick when they arrived. They were landed at Seville, where Andrés Bernáldez, the clerical chronicler, saw them put up for sale "naked as they were born." He added that they were "not very profitable since almost all died, for the country did not agree with them."

Among the captives taken to Isabela was a cacique named Guatiguaná, who escaped by gnawing through his bonds. He now tried to unite the Indians of Hispaniola, estimated to be at least 250,000 in number, against the Spaniards. But although all natives of the island were of the same race and culture, they were incapable of united action. Guacanagarí, at the northwestern end of the island, remained faithful to his unwritten treaty with Columbus, and the caciques of Xaragua and Higuey, at the other extremities, flattered themselves that they could remain neutral. Nevertheless, Guatiguaná managed to collect a formidable army in the Vega Real to march on Isabela. The Spaniards wisely did not wait there to be surrounded or overwhelmed, but took the offensive. The Admiral, Bartholomew and Hojeda marched to the Puerto de los Hidalgos with twenty horse, twenty hounds and two hundred foot, half of them armed with arquebusses. The fire from these primitive muskets alarmed the Tainos more than it harmed them, but when Hojeda charged at the head of the cavalry, dashing into the closely huddled mass of Indians, and at the same time unleashed the savage dogs, the rout became complete. This, the first pitched battle between white men and Indians, took place at the end of March, 1495.

Hojeda followed up his victory by capturing Caonabó, toughest of the caciques, who had been responsible for exterminating the Navidad garrison. He was invited to make a state visit to Isabela, and Hojeda, who conducted the cacique thither, persuaded him to wear a set of handcuffs and shackles on the representation that they were fashionable jewelry in Spain. Then the wretched Indian was thrown into the Isabela calaboose, where he fretted and grated his teeth "like a lion." Next, Hojeda subdued Caonabó's brother-in-law, the cacique of Xaragua, who was reputed to be raising an army to revenge his kindred.

The original Isabela beachhead was now expanded to cover the entire island. The Admiral himself made a triumphal march across Hispaniola, which by 1496 was so thoroughly subdued that a Spaniard could safely go wherever he pleased and help himself to the Indians' food, women and gold.

This conquest of Hispaniola was typical of the manner in which various European nations took possession of the Americas. That conquest was not effected merely by superiority of weapons. The arquebusses and field cannon of around 1500 had very feeble firepower and were not much more effective than crossbows. Some Indians who use poisoned arrows have been able to keep white men out of their fastnesses even today. Horses and dogs helped the invaders to conquer native empires, but these were not the whole story; in every instance the Europeans had native allies. It was the inability of Indians to unite, and, as regards those nearest the coast, their lack of sea power, that doomed them to eventual defeat. Europeans were always able to set one tribe against another; even Columbus had some of Guacanagarí's subjects in his fight with Guatiguaná. Occasionally (as in the case of Navidad and Belén) the natives would overwhelm a European garrison by sheer numbers, or even rush one ship with a fleet of canoes, but the white men always came back over their oceanic lifeline.

For almost a year the Columbus brothers were occupied with subjugating and organizing Hispaniola in order to obtain as much gold as possible. Several forts were built in the interior, and armed men were sent to force the natives to deliver a tribute of gold, the alternative to being killed. Every Indian fourteen years old or upward had to pay four hawks' bells full of gold dust annually; caciques had to pay about the equivalent of two hundred and twenty-five dollars, or forty-five guineas, every month. As Las Casas wrote, the system was irrational, abominable and intolerable. After the Indians had handed over the gold ornaments which they had accumulated through several generations, the only way they could get enough to pay the tribute was by continual, unremitting labor, washing grains of gold out of the gravel of streams or clearing the land of trees and sluicing it. Even after the tribute was cut down fifty per cent, it was impossible, for the most part, to fulfill. Indians took to the mountains, where the Spaniards hunted them with hounds; many who escaped their torturers died of starvation; others took cassava poison to end their miseries. Finally, as we shall relate, the tribute was commuted for the *repartimiento* system, but exploitation continued in another form. By 1508 a census showed 60,000 of the estimated 1492 population of 250,000 still alive, although the Bahamas and Cuba had been raided to obtain more slaves. Fifty years later, not 500 remained. The cruel policy initiated by Columbus and pursued by his successors resulted in complete genocide.

The calumnies of Fray Buil, Margarit and others against Columbus made their mark on the Sovereigns, who sent Juan Aguado, a colonist who had returned to Spain with Torres, to investigate the charges and report to them. He arrived at Isabela in command of four provision ships in October 1495 and at once began throwing his weight around. Columbus realized he had better return home to mend his political fences. The Spanish population of the island, mostly concentrated at Isabela, had now fallen to 630, partly owing to deaths from disease, partly because many had gone home. A large number of those left behind were sick, and all were discontented. In this rich, fertile land with beautiful climate, they were still dependent on imported provisions. Nobody unless under compulsion would trouble to sow grain, said Cuneo, because "nobody wants to live in these countries," and the favorite and most potent oath heard at Isabela was, "As God may take me to Castile, I'm telling you the truth!"

It was some time before Columbus was able to get away.

Finally, naming Bartholomew the Adelantado, or commander, in his absence and ordering him to abandon Isabela and found a new capital on the south coast, he sailed home in *Niña* on March 10, 1496.

This return from the Second Voyage was a sad contrast to the pomp, pride and superb equipment of the outward passage in 1493. *Niña's* sole consort was a fifty-ton caravel named *India*, which had been built at Isabela from the timbers of *San Juan* and *Cardera*, both wrecked in a hurricane. The two caravels were dangerously overcrowded, with 225 Spaniards and 30 Indian slaves, including the cacique Caonabó, who died at sea. Their normal crews would have numbered less than 50.

Columbus was eager to make best speed home, but not enough return passages as yet had been made for anyone to know what was the quickest route; and since he had been delayed by the long northerly sail in 1493, he decided to jump off from the Leeward Islands. That was the shortest rhumb-line route, but it turned out to be the longest in time, because the caravels had to buck head winds most of the way. They took twelve days to clear Hispaniola, and two weeks more to reach Guadeloupe, where the Admiral fortunately decided to lay in a supply of native provisions. Here, his first shore party was met by an army of Carib women armed with bows and arrows, from which everyone concluded that this was the Isle of Amazons; and such they understood it to be, from a woman they captured. She said, records Ferdinand Columbus, that "the island was only inhabited by women, and that those who would have hindered the men landing were women, except four men who were there accidentally from another island; for at a certain time in the year they come to sport, and lie with them." None of this was true, except that the women were good archers; their menfolk were then hunting elsewhere on the island, and only by capturing as hostages three boys and ten women, one of whom was a cacique's lady, were the Spaniards able to force the men to provide cassava roots. These, if properly prepared so as to eliminate the poison, as the Indians showed the Spaniards, made a nourishing and palatable bread which kept better than Indian corn meal. The lady cacique and her daughter, so Columbus declared, volunteered to accompany him to Spain, and were accepted.

On April 20, 1496, *Niña* and *India* departed Guadeloupe. We have no details of the next month's sailing except that it was very slow, and mostly beating to windward. After a month at sea all hands were put on a short allowance of six ounces of cassava bread and a cup of water per diem. About that time, providentially, they caught a westerly breeze south of the Azores, but hunger increased daily. Some Spaniards proposed eating the Indians, starting with the Caribs, who were man-eaters themselves; thus it wouldn't be a sin to pay them in their own coin! Others proposed that all the natives be thrown overboard so that they would consume no more rations. Columbus, in one of his humanitarian moods, argued that after all Caribs were people and should be treated as such; the debate was still undecided on June 8 when they made landfall on the Portuguese coast about thirty-five miles north of Cape St. Vincent, where the Admiral intended. There were several pilots on board and all thought they were still hundreds of miles from shore and hundreds of miles north of their actual position. Columbus's success at hitting the land almost "on the nose" after six weeks at sea sailing a zigzag course convinced all the seafaring tribe of his high competence at dead-reckoning navigation. The only doubts have been raised by the armchair admirals and library navigators of today.

On June 11, 1496, the last leg of Columbus's Second Voyage to America ended in the Bay of Cadiz. Every available banner was broken out and all pendants run up to make as brave an appearance as possible, but it was a sad show at best, what with the miserable Indians and Spanish passengers whom an onlooker described as wasted in their bodies and with "faces the color of saffron."

Two years and nine months had passed since the Admiral's great fleet of seventeen sail departed Cadiz, with hearts high and grandiose expectations of starting a valuable colony and locating the Emperor of China. From the point of view of the average intelligent Spaniard, all that had been a phantom, and Columbus now seemed to be an importunate and impractical dreamer. Cuba was no limb of China; anyone who talked with a member of the exploring expedition could see that. Isabela, instead of being a rich trading factory like the Portuguese Mina on the Gold Coast, was a miasmic dump which even the Columbus brothers were abandoning. Instead of the promised gold mine of the Cibao, gold was diffused in small quantities over the island and could only be produced by slave labor. Instead of golden-age simplicity and peacefulness, the natives were showing fight. Nor was there even the consoling thought that before being killed the Indians had been assured of eternal life, for none had yet been baptized, except the few brought home to Spain. And so loud and angry were the cries of returned Spaniards against the Columbus brothers that the Sovereigns must have been tempted to turn them out to grass and forget about the Indies. Possibly that is what they would have done if they had not heard that the King of Portugal was about to fit out a new expedition to India, and that even Henry VII of England was interested in finding an ocean route to Cathay.

Hispaniola must be held, if only to keep rivals out.

CHAPTER XV

The Third Voyage to America

IT WAS ALWAYS a puzzle to Columbus why things turned out so badly for him as they did. He performed his religious duties regularly; he communed with God not merely in high moments of exaltation, but daily; and surely God wanted Spain to convert the Indians to the True Faith? Why, then, did Providence frown on his undertakings? He had served the Sovereigns faithfully, respected their every wish and guarded their interests, and had won for them a new domain overseas. Why, then, did they listen to Fray Buil and send out this fellow Aguado to insult him? He had made all practical preparations, kept his ships stanch, his people healthy, and his powder dry; but now, it would seem, every Spaniard's hand was against him. Why? Why? Why? The Book of Job afforded him consolation, but no clue. Perhaps it was because he had embraced the deadly sin of pride after his First Voyage, had worn excessive apparel (as befitted the rank of admiral), had taken too much pleasure in high company, rich viands and rare vintages? Pride, to be sure, is a deadly sin. So, upon arrival at Cadiz, and ever after, Columbus assumed the coarse brown habit of a Franciscan as evidence of repentance and humility, and instead of accepting invitations to castles and palaces, he put up in religious houses with rough quarters and coarse fare. While awaiting a royal command to appear at court, he stayed with a priest named Andrés Bernáldez, chaplain to the Archbishop of Seville.

Columbus might be ostentatiously simple in his habits, but he knew very well the value of publicity to impress Spaniards, and he was far from through with the New World. So, when a gracious invitation came from the Sovereigns to visit them, he organized another impressive cavalcade. A brother of Caonabó, who had been christened "Don Diego" by Bernáldez, and another member of the cacique's family, accompanied the Admiral on muleback. Servants went ahead with cages of brightly colored parrots whose screams gave advance publicity worthy of Barnum. Whenever they approached a town, feather headdresses and golden objects were unpacked from saddlebags to adorn the Indians. "Don Diego" wore around his neck a gold collar weighing the equivalent of 90 double eagles, or 360 guineas, and on his head the crown of Caonabó. It was "very big and tall, with wings on its sides like a shield and golden eyes as large as silver cups," and on it was carved a repulsive semihuman which Bernáldez, to whom we owe this description, assumed to be the devil. Unfortunately, none of these priceless objects brought home by Columbus were preserved; all were melted down. But many others of the kind have been dug up in Caribbean countries and may be seen in the museums of Europe and America.

Columbus found the King and Queen at Valladolid, and his two sons, Diego and Ferdinand, now pages to the Queen, were there to greet him. He was courteously received, especially after presenting the Sovereigns with a clutch of gold nuggets as big as pigeons' eggs. Promptly he put in a plea to be outfitted for a Third Voyage. Five ships he wanted to be laden with provisions for Hispaniola and three for himself, to seek out a continent which, as he put it, the King of Portugal believed to be in the Ocean south or southeast of the Antilles, and the existence of which had been confirmed by hints received from the Indians.

John II of Portugal, well read and intelligent in geographical matters, had evidently been impressed by such writers as Vincent of Beauvais and Isidore of Seville, who postulated a fourth part of the world, the Antipodes, south of the Equator, to "balance" Africa. John was dead, but the fact that he believed in the existence of such a continent was an incentive for Ferdinand and Isabella to get there first, and they knew that John's successor, Manuel the Fortunate, was fitting out a big overseas expedition. It seems significant that Columbus could get nothing but promises out of the Sovereigns until news from Portugal indicated that Vasco da Gama was almost ready to depart. His destination was secret; he might well be looking for the "fourth part of the world."

Between the end of April and the middle of June, 1497, Ferdinand and Isabella confirmed Columbus's rights, titles and privileges, and ordered him to recruit three hundred colonists for Hispaniola at the royal expense. Wages started at about fourteen cents a day for a common workman or soldier and rose to forty-two gold dollars a year for farmers and gardeners, plus eight cents a day for keep. Also, Columbus was authorized to recruit thirty women for the expedition; they got neither pay nor keep, but were expected to work their passage, and marry upon arrival. Unless (as there is some reason to believe) Torres brought a few women to Hispaniola in 1495, these ladies were the first Christian women to go to the New World. And the Sovereigns offered a free pardon to all malefactors confined in jail, except those guilty of major crimes like treason and heresy, if they would accompany the Admiral to the Indies and stay a year or two. Hispaniola had been so discredited that this was supposed to be the only way to get emigrants to the future "Land of Promise." Columbus sent these fellows directly to Hispaniola, which he later had reason to regret.

Another twelvemonth elapsed before Columbus was able to

complete his preparations because the Sovereigns, long on promises, were short of cash, and nobody except the jailbirds would engage for Hispaniola without advance pay. Part of the money was raised by the sale of a cargo of Indian slaves that Peralonso Niño brought back in 1496.

Niña and *India* left for Hispaniola in January 1498. Three more caravels, whose names we do not know, were chartered to sail directly to Hispaniola with supplies. They were under the tactical command of Alonso de Carvajal, who had left his job as mayor of Baeza to command a ship on the Second Voyage, and who became one of Columbus's most faithful captains. The three vessels which the Admiral reserved for his own voyage of discovery were two caravels and the flagship, about the size of the original *Santa María*. He never referred to her by name, but called her *La Nao* (the Ship) to distinguish her from the other two. The larger caravel, measuring 70 tons, was called *La Vaqueños*, and the smaller and swifter one, *El Correo*. The Admiral encountered great difficulties in equipping this small fleet because most of it had to be done on credit. He had numerous rows with Fonseca, who had immediate charge of preparations, and on one occasion became so exasperated with a rascally ship chandler that he knocked him down.

Columbus's three vessels and the three under Carvajal assembled at Seville and departed during the last week of May, 1498 — the same week that Vasco da Gama arrived at Calicut in India. All six dropped down the Guadalquivir to the roadstead of Sanlúcar de Barrameda, where the Admiral came on board, and on May 30 the Third Voyage to America began.

This time, Columbus decided to sail a more southerly cours than before, both to discover King John's continent and to seek more gold; for as we have seen, it was a persistent superstition that all precious things were to be found near the Equator. So he planned to drop down to the supposed latitude of Sierra Leone, where the Portuguese had found their Guinea gold, and sail due west. The Admiral knew very well that he must accomplish something spectacular on this voyage or the whole Enterprise of the Indies might be abandoned. He sometimes compared himself to David, who was commanded to perform incredible tasks and did so, but each time fell into greater disfavor with Saul. He had discovered a western route to "the Indies," but that was not enough. He had led a great fleet to Hispaniola, founded a colony there, discovered the Lesser Antilles, Puerto Rico and Jamaica and explored Cuba, but that was not enough. He must now discover more gold and a continent (which he did — but even that was not enough). Of course he could have retired after his return from the Second Voyage with a title, a castle and a pension, and left Bartholomew or someone else to rule Hispaniola, but he was not the kind of man to sell out; if he had been, we should never have heard of him.

His first port of call on this voyage was Funchal, Madeira, where he had resided for a time in his young manhood, and where he was now received as a hero. He then made a three-day run to the familiar roadstead of San Sebastián, Gomera. Evidently the romance with Doña Beatriz was completely dead, since all that Columbus or anyone else wrote about this call at her capital was, "We took on cheeses."

At Gomera, Carvajal's Hispaniola squadron of three caravels, one of them commanded by the Admiral's cousin Giannetto Colombo, parted company with the exploring squadron. Columbus gave them their course, West and by South to Dominica. They made that landfall as directed, but afterward got into trouble, as we shall see.

From the Canaries, Columbus set a course for the Cape Verde Islands, making 750 miles in six days. He made a brief stop at

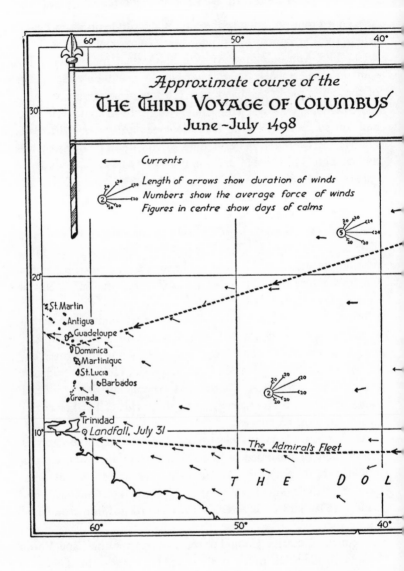

Approximate course of the
THE THIRD VOYAGE OF COLUMBUS
June – July 1498

Currents

Length of arrows show duration of winds
Numbers show the average force of winds
Figures in centre show days of calms

St. Martin
Antigua
Guadeloupe
Dominica
Martinique
St. Lucia
Barbados
Grenada
Trinidad
Landfall, July 31

The Admiral's Fleet

T H E D O L

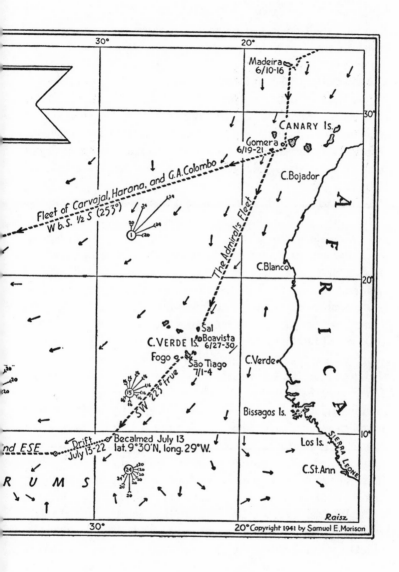

30°   20°

Madeira
6/10-16

CANARY IS.

Gomera
6/19-21

C.Bojador

A F R I C A

Fleet of Carvajal, Harana, and G.A.Colombo
W.b.S. ½ S (253°)

The Admiral's Fleet

C.Blanco

30°

20°

Sal
Boavista
6/27-30

C.VERDE IS.

Fogo

São Tiago
7/1-4

C.Verde

SW 223° true

Bissagos Is.

Los Is.

C.St.Ann

SIERRA LEONE

10°

nd ESE   Drift
July 13-22   Becalmed July 13
lat. 9°30'N, long. 29°W.

R U M S

30°   20° Copyright 1941 by Samuel E. Morison

Raisz

Boavista to salt down goat mutton, the only meat that the island afforded; then, on July 1, called at São Tiago in the hope of obtaining some live cattle to breed in Hispaniola. After staying a week there in heat so intense that many of his people fell ill, he departed without the cattle. The vessels were becalmed for three days within sight of Fogo, but on July 7 the trades sprang up. Columbus shaped a course southwest, seeking the parallel of Sierra Leone. But the wind grew more and more soft, and finally died completely on July 13 when the fleet had reached about latitude 9 degrees 30 minutes North, longitude 29 degrees West.

Columbus was in the doldrums, and for the next eight days his vessels drifted with the equatorial current, while their crews, who would have thought it suicidal to strip down and get tanned, sweltered in their thick woolen clothes. The Admiral profited (as he thought) from the calm to observe the North Star with his quadrant, but as usual in his efforts at celestial navigation, he made so many mistakes that he found the latitude to be 5 degrees North, over 250 miles too far south. He was pleased to believe that he had reached 5 degrees North for a curious reason. Many years before, one of King John's Portuguese navigators had taken the latitude of the Los Islands off the coast of Sierra Leone and found it to be 5 degrees North, as Columbus had heard. The amusing thing is that the Portuguese navigator reached the same mistaken result that Columbus did; the true latitude of the Los Islands is 9 degrees 30 minutes North, very close to what Columbus's fleet actually attained! So the Admiral really was where he wished to be, and the only result of his four-and-a-half-degree error was to throw off all his subsequent calculations of latitude.

On July 22, 1498, a fresh trade wind sprang up from the east-southeast, slack lines became taut, limp sails bellied out, the ships quickly got under way, the temperature dropped, and the sailors, who had half expected to rot and die in mid-ocean (for none had before experienced whole days of calm), began talking about the gold they were going to find. The Admiral set the course due west, and for nine days, with a prosperous blast from the trade wind, his fleet made an average speed of six knots or better.

This leg of the voyage must have been almost pure delight to the Admiral and his men; we know that, as we followed the same route in our *Capitana*. Day and night the fleet made wonderful speed. In the trades, vessels always roll a good deal, but the fair and steady wind singing in the rigging, the sapphire white-capped sea, the rush of great waters alongside, and the endless succession of puffy trade-wind clouds lift a seaman's spirits and make him want to shout and sing. The old-time Spanish mariners called these broad waters El Golfo de las Damas, The Ladies' Sea, so easy is the navigation, so mild and genial the climate. Occasionally a black squall makes up from windward, but passes harmlessly with a brief lash of rain. For days the sheets and braces need no attention except to alter the nip on the block so that they will not chafe through. Flying fish and dorados play about the ship, and the pelagic birds, petrels and the like, pay brief visits. On moonless nights the sails stand out black against the star-studded firmament, and as the ship makes her southing, new stars and constellations appear — Canopus, Capricorn, Argo with her False Cross, and the true Southern Cross. Columbus had already seen *Crux Australis* from Hispaniola in winter, but most of his men were new to southern waters, and one can imagine them, as in Heredia's famous sonnet, leaning entranced over the bulwarks of the caravels and seeing in the phosphorescent sea an augury of the gold of the Indies.

Sailors can always find something to grumble about and now it was the continual fair wind. How will we ever get back to Spain if we go on this way? said they. But even though the Ad-

miral's latitude was screwy, he was keeping a good dead reckoning and knew almost exactly where he was, relative to the discoveries of the Second Voyage. On July 31 he announced that
he was on the meridian of the Lesser Antilles, which was correct,
and, since the supply of fresh water was dangerously low, he
decided to make a northern detour to water up in Dominica
or some other Caribbee isle. That very morning he altered the
course to North by East, which, if continued would have taken
the fleet to Barbados or Tobago.

At noon the Admiral's servant Alonso Pérez, having gone aloft,
sang out that he saw land to the westward in the form of three
hills. We, in our *Capitana*, reached a position within a mile or
two of the one where Columbus made that landfall, twenty days
out from the Canaries. Our lookout aloft shouted, "Three hills
dead ahead, sir!" A rainsquall then blotted them out, but in another hour we had the pleasure of seeing from the deck the
same hills which, on the last day of July, 1498, seemed to Columbus a happy omen. He had placed this voyage under the special
protection of the Holy Trinity, so without hesitation he named
the island Trinidad.

The Admiral changed course to approach the land. Before long
he could see the southeastern point of the island, which he named
Cabo de la Galera[1] because its peaked cliffs resemble lateen
sails and diagonal marks on the rock look like a bank of oars.
The caravels arrived off this cape about 9 P.M., and as the moon
was nearly full, jogged westward all night.

Next day, the first of August, the Admiral continued along
the south coast of Trinidad, searching for a bay that would have
a river emptying into it. With his usual good judgment in such

[1] This name, through a misunderstanding of Columbus's landfall, has been
transferred to the northeast point of Trinidad; Columbus's landfall is now
called Galeota Point.

matters, he chose the best watering place on that coast, now called Erin Bay, where a stream of cool, sweet water crosses the beach. The men went ashore, washed their clothes, wallowed in the fresh water to sluice the caked salt and sweat from their bodies, and had a fine time splashing and yelling, and hallooing into the jungle in the hope that some pretty native girls might respond.

Just before hauling into Erin Bay, Columbus had his first sight of the South American continent, without knowing it. He saw a low cape which we have identified as Bombeador Point, Venezuela, but he thought it was just another island.

As the anchorage in Erin Bay affords slight protection from the trades, Columbus weighed on August 2 and sailed through the Boca de la Sierpe into the great Gulf of Paria that lies between Trinidad and the mainland. He must have sailed through the Boca at slack water, as he made no remark about the current that swirls so dangerously around the mid-channel rock as to embarrass even steamers. Columbus anchored in the lee of Icacos Point, Trinidad, and ordered all hands ashore in relays for a few days' relaxation. They amused themselves fishing and gathering oysters, while the Admiral caused the Boca to be sounded, and marveled at the speed and fury of the current at full flood or ebb.

The only contact with the natives at this point was both comic and pathetic. Columbus had been hoping and praying that this time he would encounter either Chinese mandarins or Negro potentates like those on the Gold Coast. But when a dugout canoe approached, he observed with disgust that it contained only naked male Indians looking much the same as Caribs, but, fortunately, with better manners. He derived some consolation from the fact that they wore cotton bandannas like those obtained by the Portuguese in Sierra Leone. With this apparent confirmation of Aristotle's theory of the same latitude producing

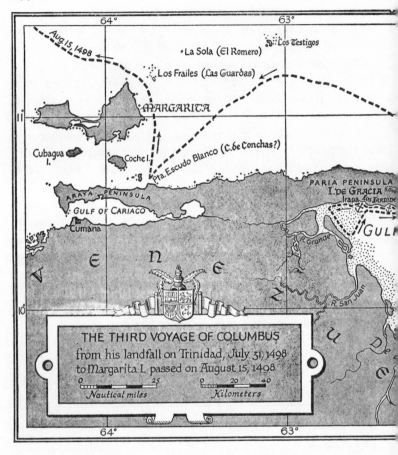

THE THIRD VOYAGE OF COLUMBUS
from his landfall on Trinidad, July 31, 1498
to Margarita I. passed on August 15, 1498

the same things the world over, he was sure to find Guinea gold around the corner! The Admiral, hoping to start trade, caused some brass chamber pots and other shining objects to be enticingly displayed over the bulwarks, but the Trinidad Indians were not impressed by these common objects of the European home. Next, the Admiral tried putting on a show for their bene-

fit; he ordered a pipe-and-tabor player to sound off, tambourines to be jingled, and the ships' boys to dance. The Indians evidently took this as a warming-up for a fight and let fly a shower of arrows, none of which hit. And that was all that the Spaniards saw of the natives of Trinidad.

CHAPTER XVI

An Other World

ON AUGUST 4, as the caravels were weighing anchor and about to square away to explore the gulf, the Spaniards had probably the greatest fright of their lives. An enormous bore or tidal wave, evidently caused by a volcanic disturbance, roared through the Boca, snapped the anchor rode of *Vaqueños*, raised the flagship to what seemed an immense height, and dropped her so low that one could see bottom. The Admiral decided that this was no place to stay and named the strait La Boca de la Sierpe, The Serpent's Mouth.

Attracted by the sight of mountains of the Paria Peninsula across the gulf, Columbus now steered due north. As he approached the end of the peninsula, he enjoyed the same gorgeous view that greets a sailor today. Astern lay the placid gulf, its far shores below the horizon; westward under the setting sun stretched a succession of mountains and rugged headlands; eastward were the high, broken islands that divide the famous Bocas del Dragón, and behind them rose the mountains of Trinidad, range after range. And far to the northeast, as it was a very clear evening, Columbus sighted an island which must have been Tobago. After a library navigator had figured out that he couldn't possibly have seen Tobago, we sighted it in 1940 from the topgallant yard of our *Capitana* when in a position very near the Admiral's in 1498!

Columbus anchored for the night at Bahía Celeste near the tip of the peninsula and next day started to explore its southern shore along the gulf. Here are many harbors, and the most attractive, Ensenada Yacua, a little round cove with a sand beach between two rocky headlands, is probably the one that Columbus chose for a landing. He found a large thatched house and a fire burning, but the natives had fled, their places taken by swarms of monkeys who chattered indignantly at the Spaniards. This was the first place where Columbus or his men set foot on the mainland of America; the first time, indeed, that any European had done so since the Vinland voyages, unless John Cabot had reached Nova Scotia the previous summer, which is possible. As was usual with the Admiral, he did not know what he had discovered; he still believed that Paria Peninsula was an island. The date was Sunday, August 5, 1498.

Since it would have been undignified to take formal possession for Spain with no other audience than monkeys, Columbus postponed the ceremony until two days later when a horde of friendly natives appeared at the mouth of the Rio Guiria. The Admiral himself was suffering severely from sore eyes, so he stayed on board and sent his senior captain, Pedro de Terreros, veteran of the first two voyages, to take formal possession of this "Province," which the Indians told him was called Paria.

After a preliminary distribution of beads, sugar and hawks' bells, the Indians came out in a fleet of canoes bringing fruits of the country and a beer called *chicha* fermented from maize, which is still brewed in Venezuela. They wore as ornaments great polished disks made of an alloy of copper and gold that they called *guanin* and which modern archaelogists have named *tumbaga*. By smelting copper with gold the melting point was reduced from over a thousand degrees centigrade to about eight hundred, a great advantage to these primitive metallurgists, and as they had to import the copper from Central America, it was more valuable to them than gold. So, greatly to the Spaniards' delight, these natives of Paria were willing to swap objects of which the greater part was gold for their weight in brass or copper. Columbus had not only found the mainland but entered a new area of native culture, which extends from the Guianas to Honduras.

On August 8 the fleet resumed the exploration of the gulf, rounded the long, tapering Punta Alcatraz (which Columbus called Aguja, the Needle) and found a rich lowland with gardens and groves of big, glossy-leaved mahogany and fustic trees which he named Los Jardines, The Gardens. The women of one village came on board wearing necklaces of fine pearls which Columbus ascertained came from the other side of the peninsula. That caused great excitement among the Spaniards, not only for the value of the pearls, but because pearls meant the Orient. The Indians were willing to sell what pearls they had for the usual trading truck, but unfortunately they had no spares; so the Admiral begged them by sign language to accumulate a few bushels of them against his return; but return he never did. The natives at this pleasant place were so friendly that a whole boat's crew accepted an invitation to a feast in a big thatched house, and returned to the ship fat and happy.

Again the Admiral turned west in search of an outlet to the sea. The water, already brackish, shoaled and became fresh and turbid. Caravel *Correo*, sent ahead to reconnoiter because of her light draft, reported four river channels to the westward. These were the mouths of the Rio Grande, and a mouth of the Orinoco emptied a few miles away. Columbus, stubborn as usual in his geographical ideas, was not yet convinced that this was a river or that he was exploring mainland. But he gave up the search for an outlet that wasn't there and turned east again at the rising of the moon on August 11.

The land breeze held all day, and with a favoring current from the rivers he reached the Bocas the same night and anchored in a harbor that he named Puerto de Gatos (Monkey Harbor) on Chacachacare Island. In the small hours of the thirteenth, the fleet weighed and stood into Boca Grande. There they found the usual turmoil between the fresh water flowing out and the salt tide roaring in, and "thought to perish" when the wind dropped and the caravels drifted toward the rocks; but the fresh water prevailed over the salt, and they were slowly carried out, and to safety. Columbus named this strait Boca del Dragón because they had escaped, as it were, the dragon's mouth, and the name is still used for all four channels that connect the Gulf of Paria with the Caribbean. Dangerous they still are for small craft.

On the way out Columbus sighted to the northward, over sixty miles distant, the island of Grenada and named it Asunción because it was the vigil of the Feast of the Assumption. At dawn August 15 he sighted an island that he named Margarita (as it is still called), but he did not tarry to look for the pearls that were there in abundance, as he was in a great hurry to get to Santo Domingo. That decision, as it turned out, was a mistake. Discovery of the Pearl Coast would have helped his prestige at home; conditions in Hispaniola would have been no worse if he had stayed another month. Again, each of his rôles of discoverer and colonial administrator hurt the other.

It was on this Feast of the Assumption that it suddenly dawned on the Admiral just what Paria was. In his Journal he recorded, "I believe that this is a very great continent, until today unknown. And reason aids me greatly because of that so great river and fresh-water sea, and next, the saying of Esdras . . . that the six parts of the world are of dry land, and one of water. . . . Which book of Esdras St. Ambrose approved in his *Examenon* and so St. Augustine in the passage *morietur filius meus Chris-*

tus, as Francisco de Mayrones alleges; and further I am supported by the sayings of many Carib Indians whom I took at other times, who said that to the south of them was mainland . . . and they said that in it there was much gold. . . . And if this be a continent, it is a marvelous thing, and will be so among all the wise, since so great a river flows that it makes a fresh-water sea of 48 leagues."

This passage, "his very words," we are assured by Las Casas, is typical of the workings of Columbus's mind. For two weeks he had been sailing along the coast of the continent that he sought, yet refused to believe that it was one because it did not match his idea of a continent. Finally, the evidence of the vast volume of fresh water changed his mind, and at once the old Esdras "six parts out of seven," odd scraps of scholastic learning, and vague gestures of Caribs flew together in his mind to prove it.

These lands, he said, are an Other World (*otro mundo*), as indeed they were. It was mere chance that he did not write *nuevo mundo,* New World, which would have entitled him to the credit afterwards granted to Amerigo Vespucci of having recognized it as such. Actually the two phrases, as Columbus and Vespucci used them (and as Peter Martyr had already used *mundus novus*), meant the same thing, a region hitherto unknown to Europeans, or not mentioned in Ptolemy's Geography. It distinctly did not mean the "New World" that we use to denote the Americas. Columbus believed that the mainland he had just coasted along was in the same relation to China and the Malay Peninsula as is the present Republic of Indonesia.

But Columbus was not satisfied to make two and two equal four; they must make twenty-two. A couple of days later he confided to his Journal that this continent was the Terrestrial Paradise, the Garden of Eden! Several medieval writers quoted in Columbus's favorite bedside book, *Imago Mundi,* on the basis of Genesis ii 8, "The Lord God planted a garden eastward in Eden," placed that famous garden at the farthest point of the Far East, where the sun rose on the day of creation. Turning again to the second chapter of Genesis, Columbus read of trees "pleasant to the sight and good for food," and of the river with "four heads" that watered the garden, and caravel *Correo* had reported four mouths. "And the gold of that land is good" — it certainly was, even though the silly natives liked copper better. Wasn't it striking how that chapter of Genesis described the Gulf of Paria? Yet even this did not exhaust the Admiral's imagination. He jumped from some wildly inaccurate deductions he had made of the North Star's elevation on this voyage to the still more amazing conclusion that the globe at this point had a bump on it like a woman's breast, in order to bring the Terrestrial Paradise nearer Heaven! Did not the violent currents in the Bocas prove that the water was running downhill?

Although Columbus was suffering from arthritis and inflamed eyes, he was not out of his mind, as these weird conclusions might suggest; equally strange hypotheses were common among discoverers and stay-at-home geographers in that era. Through it all he kept accurate dead reckoning of his daily positions. From Margarita on August 15 he set a course Northwest by North for Saona Island off Hispaniola, as a good point whence to coast downwind to Santo Domingo, the new island capital. And that *was* the correct air-line course! Imagine all the factors Columbus had to feed into his mental computer to get this result — Hispaniola to Cape St. Vincent and Cadiz in 1496; Sanlúcar to Madeira, Gomera and the Cape Verdes in 1498; São Tiago to latitude 9 degrees 30 minutes North, and then West, and through the Gulf of Paria and to Margarita. How he did it I cannot explain.

Although Northwest by North was the direct course to Saona,

two factors prevented Columbus from making it. One, beyond the Admiral's knowledge or control, was the westward-running equatorial current, which he had no means of gauging; the other, due to his very proper fear of running on reefs in the dark of the moon, was his cautious navigation, which lengthened the passage and so increased his set to leeward. He ordered the caravels to jog or heave-to every night, heaving the lead frequently, and to make sail only by day when dangerous reefs could be detected by changes in the color of the water. The result was that Columbus made landfall on Alta Vela, 120 miles southwest of Santo Domingo. "It weighed on him to have fallen off so much," wrote Las Casas, but he decided correctly that his miscalculation was caused by a strong current. How would any modern navigator fare over the course of the Third Voyage without charts, without a log line, with no means for accurate check by celestial bodies? Remember, all land touched at after the Cape Verdes was newly discovered, and no ship had been spoken since the first of July. Could any of us, under such conditions, have figured out the correct course from Margarita Island, Venezuela, to Santo Domingo? If this was not superb dead reckoning, it was divine guidance; perhaps a combination of the two!

On August 21, anchored in the shelter of Beata Island (which the Admiral named Madama Beata, the Blessed Lady), Columbus saw a little caravel approaching from the direction of Santo Domingo. The stranger fired a gun, luffed up alongside the flagship, and to the Admiral's delight he was hailed by brother Bartholomew. The Adelantado was engaged in pursuing the provision squadron under Carvajal, which had been sighted from shore, but had stupidly missed Santo Domingo. After this happy reunion the four caravels beat up to the new capital town in eight days, which was thought to be very good going against wind and current.

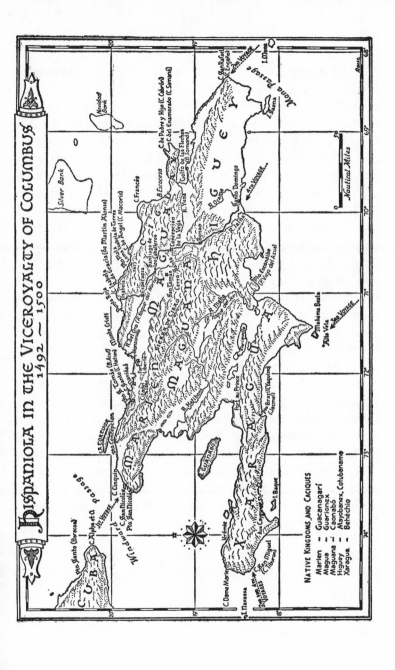

Hispaniola in the Viceroyalty of Columbus 1492 – 1500

NATIVE KINGDOMS AND CACIQUES

Marien – Guacanagarí
Magua – Guarionex
Maguana – Caonabó
Higuey – Mayobanex, Cotubanamá
Xaragua. – Behéchio

Nautical Miles

To all intents and purposes, Columbus's Third Voyage ended August 31, 1498, when *La Nao, Correo* and *Vaqueños* anchored in the Ozama River, the present inner harbor of Ciudad Trujillo. Another voyage had been brilliantly carried through. The Admiral had found the gateway to a vast territory for the expansion of the Spanish race, language and culture, extending from the Rocky Mountains to the Straits of Magellan. What matter if he did think it was the Garden of Eden? Note what he wrote in his Journal of this voyage, on the day he reached farthest west in the Gulf of Paria: "It would be the greatest thing for Spain to have a revenue from this undertaking; your Highnesses could leave nothing of greater memory. . . . And your Highnesses will gain these vast lands, which are an Other World, and where Christianity will have so much enjoyment, and our faith in time so great an increase. I say this with very honest intent and because I desire that your Highnesses may be the greatest lords in the world, lords of it all, I say; and that all may be with much service to and satisfaction of the Holy Trinity."

Superb faith; marvelous prophecy! At a time when Spain's first overseas colony was languishing, and settlers had to be recruited from the jails; when few people of any importance believed in Columbus or thought his discoveries worth the smallest of the Canary Islands, he foretold the vast revenue that Spain would obtain from these conquests, making her the first power in Europe; he predicted that Christianity, whose territory had been shrinking since the rise of Islam, would advance triumphantly into his Other and New World.

CHAPTER XVII

Admiral of the Mosquitos

THE CONTRAST between the terrestrial paradise of Paria and the very special hell that Hispaniola had become was profound and distressing. The only good news for Columbus was the abandonment of hateful and unhealthy Isabela and the founding of Santo Domingo; Bartholomew had managed the transfer with ability and dispatch. Santo Domingo was still a city of palm thatch and wattle, but it was well sited at the mouth of a large river with an ample roadstead and well-protected harbor. Renamed Ciudad Trujillo, it is now the capital of the Dominican Republic and one of the leading cities of the Caribbean.

The worst news was the rebellion led by Francisco Roldán, whom the Admiral had appointed chief justice of Hispaniola. Roldán, a true demagogue, promised all things to all men; to the Spaniards, more gold, more slaves, more food from Spain, passage home to all who wished it and freedom from the hated rule of the Genoese; to the Indians, less work and no more tribute or slave raids. Guarionex, the cacique of Maguana, and the Ciguayos of the Samaná peninsula joined Roldán. Bartholomew subdued them first. When he was ready to deal with Roldán, the rebel leader with about seventy armed men retreated to Xaragua, the southwest peninsula of the island. There then occurred a most unfortunate break for the administration. Carvajal's three caravels, which had missed Santo Domingo, fetched up at Roldán's headquarters on the coast of Xaragua. Carvajal was steadfastly loyal to Columbus, but the former jailbirds among his passengers and some of the other recruits swarmed ashore and flocked to the rebel standard. Roldán, thus reinforced, marched on the fortress of La Vega in the center of the island. As many of the loyal Spaniards at Santo Domingo were down with syphilis or other diseases, the Columbus brothers were unable to muster an army of equal size and dared not risk a battle. They tried appeasement.

After almost a year of parleying, in which Roldán constantly raised his terms, Columbus restored the rebel to his office of chief justice, proclaimed that all charges against him were baseless, promised free passage home with gold and slaves to those of his followers who wished to leave and land grants in Xaragua to those who wished to stay.

As part of this settlement with Roldán, and in favor both of rebels and loyalists, Columbus abandoned the last vestiges of his trading-factory colonial policy and adopted the system of *repartimientos*, which eventually spread through a large part of Spanish America. This meant that a Spanish settler was allotted a plot of cultivated land and at the same time was assigned, as his personal slaves, the Indians who lived on it. The caciques consented to this blow to their authority as the means of getting rid of the intolerable gold tribute, and the Spaniards liked it since it provided them with free labor and guaranteed them all the gold they could find on their plots, less the Crown's and the Admiral's percentages. *Repartimientos* did not at once make the colony pay, or save Columbus from disgrace, but they did abolish the cruel gold tribute and induce colonists to settle down.

Other problems were crowding upon the Admiral. Nothing was more clear in his original contract than his complete authority as Viceroy and Governor over such lands as he might discover, and his complete control over trade with or exploration of them.

But when his flagship and *Correo* returned to Spain in the fall of 1498 (he retained only *Vaqueños* at Santo Domingo), Alonso de Hojeda got possession of the journal and chart that Columbus sent to the Sovereigns and obtained a license to make an independent voyage to Paria to search for pearls. He took with him the map maker Juan de la Cosa and a clever Florentine resident at Seville named Amerigo Vespucci, whose amusing account of this voyage, predated two years, led a North European geographer to name the continent America. Hojeda picked up the route of Columbus's Third Voyage along the Spanish Main from the point near Margarita where he had broken off, collected a large number of pearls, discovered Aruba and Curaçao and the Gulf of Maracaibo (which he named Venezuela, Little Venice, from the native villages on piles), called at Xaragua, where he first joined with Roldán and then quarreled with him, made a slave raid on the Bahamas, and finally returned to Spain. All this in the year 1499 and early 1500. In the latter year, Peralonso Niño, former pilot of *Santa María*, made a rich haul of pearls, and Vicente Yáñez Pinzón, former captain of *Niña*, discovered the mouth of the Amazon. Pretty soon every ambitious conquistador would be fitting out a voyage to America without Columbus's knowledge or consent.

At court, in the meantime, the Admiral's stock was falling. Complaints against the rule of the Columbus family were accumulating. Spaniards who returned from the Indies were making nuisances of themselves, assaulting the King whenever he stirred abroad with cries of "Pay! Pay!" Ferdinand Columbus recorded how he and his brother Diego, pages to the Queen, were mortified by these wretches hooting at them and shouting, "There go the sons of the Admiral of the Mosquitos, of him who discovered lands of vanity and delusion, the ruin and the grave of Castilian gentlemen!"

Yet it must be admitted that as administrators the three Columbus brothers had been failures. They had been weak when they should have been firm, and ruthless at the wrong time; they had not saved the Indians from exploitation, and had alienated most of the Spaniards, especially by using their control over imported provisions as a means of reward and punishment. The Sovereigns, before receiving news that Roldán had made peace and that the *repartimiento* reform had been adopted, appointed Francisco de Bobadilla to go to Hispaniola as royal commissioner, with unlimited powers over persons and property. If Bobadilla had sailed immediately, he would have arrived when matters were peaceful and the Columbus brothers were doing fairly well. Unfortunately for them, his departure was delayed for over a year, and he arrived at Santo Domingo on August 23, 1500, when the Admiral was at La Vega, Bartholomew at Xaragua, and the weak Diego in charge of the city. Upon landing, the first thing that Bobadilla saw was a gallows from which were hanging seven Spanish corpses, and Diego cheerfully remarked that five more were due to be hanged next day. These men had rebelled under one Adrián de Moxica and had been defeated and captured with Roldán's assistance. Bobadilla was shocked; without waiting to hear the Columbus side of the affair, he took over the fort and the government, tossed Don Diego into the brig of his flagship, impounded all the Admiral's effects, won over the populace by proclaiming a general freedom to gather gold anywhere, and when the Admiral appeared in obedience to his summons, he too was chained and confined in the town calaboose. Bartholomew, then in the interior with a loyal army, might have marched on the capital and released his brothers, but the Admiral neither dared nor cared to defy the royal authority that Bobadilla represented. On his advice, Bartholomew, too, submitted and received his share of fetters.

Bobadilla, after compiling a file of anti-Columbus depositions from all the discontented and mutinous Spaniards, decided to send the three brothers home for trial. In early October the Admiral and Diego, both chained and without any of their gold or other property, were placed on board caravel *La Gorda*, bound for Spain; Bartholomew was sent in another vessel. The captain of *La Gorda* "would have knocked off the Admiral's irons," says son Ferdinand, "but he would not permit it, saying that they had been put on him by regal authority, and only the Sovereigns could order them struck off."

Christopher Columbus was a sensitive gentleman to whom these indignities were far more humiliating than they would have been to the average tough *hombre* of that era. On his way home he wrote to a true friend at court, Doña Juana de Torres, a long letter which is at once a cry of distress, a bill of complaints and a proud vindication of his own conduct. Our Lord, he said, had made him the messenger of the "new heaven and new earth" envisioned in the Apocalypse and prophesied in the sixty-fifth chapter of Isaiah. The Queen, to whom God had given understanding of what Columbus was about, had, as a reward, been made heiress to this Other World, and in her name he went out and took possession. Yet there is none of her subjects so vile that he cannot now insult the Admiral with impunity. He is accused of illegal actions, but he has put down two rebellions against the Sovereigns' authority, and how can one deal with armed men by due process of law? He has safeguarded their Highnesses' interests in the collection of gold. Then Bobadilla arrives, listens to the calumnies of rogues, throws him and his brothers into jail for their alleged breach of legality, and removes all restrictions on gold collections so that one rascal made thirty guineas' worth in four hours! Columbus ended with a poignant expression of outraged dignity and sense of justice:

In Spain they judge me as a governor who had gone to Sicily or to a city or town under a regular government, where the laws can be observed *in toto* without fear of losing all. . . . I should be judged as a captain who went from Spain to the Indies to conquer a people numerous and warlike whose manners and religion are very different from ours . . . and where by the divine will I have placed under the sovereignty of the King and Queen an Other World, whereby Spain, which was reckoned poor, is become the richest of countries. . . .

God our Lord is present with His strength and wisdom, as of old, and in the end especially punisheth ingratitude and injuries.

Fair winds attended the voyage home of *La Gorda*, as if the Ocean Sea had wished to shorten the miseries of her Admiral. Before the end of October he was set ashore at Cadiz, and, still in chains and accompanied by his jailer, went to stay at the monastery of Las Cuevas in Seville. The spectacle of Columbus in chains is said to have made a lamentable impression on the populace, but six weeks elapsed before the Sovereigns ordered him released from his fetters and summoned him to court.

The three brothers presented themselves to the King and Queen at the Alhambra in Granada shortly before Christmas, 1500. Don Diego, now in his twenty-first year, was there, too, and son Ferdinand, a boy of twelve. As courtiers they must have been deeply mortified to see their now aged and ailing father dressed in Franciscan brown and with marks of iron fetters on his ankles and wrists. Thereafter the Admiral kept the fetters in his chamber, as a gloomy souvenir of his humiliation, and ordered that they be buried with him.

The Sovereigns spoke to Columbus in a kindly and consoling manner, and promised that justice would be done and his privileges restored. Weeks stretched into months, but nothing happened. There was always more urgent business than the affairs of distant Hispaniola to occupy the Sovereigns' attention. First it was the partition of Naples with France; then it was the departure of the fifteen-year-old Infanta Caterina to marry the Prince of Wales. In the meantime, Bastidas, Peralonso Niño, Hojeda and others were making voyages on their own along the coast of the "Other World."

Columbus wanted complete restoration of his rights, properties, titles and offices. He spent a great deal of time and effort compiling a Book of Privileges, containing all his agreements with and orders and letters from the Sovereigns. But it was hopeless for him to expect to get everything back. He and his brothers had made too much of a mess of things in Hispaniola to be given the government again, and now that the coast of South America was being opened up, it was idle to suppose that the Sovereigns would confirm tithes and similar privileges over a continent that had originally been granted on presumption of a trading factory and a few islands. Again, Columbus would have been well advised to settle for a reasonable dignity and security, such as a castle, a pension and a ducal title; there was no objection to his continuing to style himself Viceroy and Admiral, only to his exercising those functions. But he was not the man to give anything up. Had he been, he would never have discovered America.

In September 1501, after waiting eight months, Columbus learned the worst. Instead of his being sent back in triumph to Hispaniola, Bobadilla was merely recalled and Don Nicolás de Ovando was appointed Governor of the Islands and Mainlands of the Indies. Columbus did obtain these concessions: permission to retain his now empty titles of Viceroy and Admiral and to send out an agent in Ovando's fleet to make Bobadilla disgorge the moneys due him. And perhaps it was some consolation that the Sovereigns had now decided that the Enterprise of the Indies must go on. Ovando departed in February 1502 with a magnificent fleet of thirty sail, carrying twenty-five hundred sailors, soldiers and colonists.

Impatient to embark once more on his proper element, and convinced that nothing was to be gained by hanging about the court or bombarding it with petitions, Columbus now asked for money and ships to make a fourth voyage to the Indies. The Sovereigns so ordered, only a month after Ovando sailed for Hispaniola.

CHAPTER XVIII

The High Voyage

COLUMBUS'S FOURTH and last Voyage to America is in many respects the most interesting, and he evidently thought so, too, as he always referred to it, in the short span of life that remained to him, as El Alto Viaje, The High Voyage. Almost fifty-one years old at the start of it, and fifty-three when he returned, the Admiral was already an old man by the standards of the day, but in this voyage he showed the highest quality of seamanship, superb courage and complete fitness to command. One only regrets that he did not altogether escape administrative problems, because the Treasurer of Castile, on whom he depended for everyone's pay, insisted on his taking the two Porras brothers as captain of a caravel and crown comptroller, since their sister was his mistress. An odd way of pleasing a mistress, but that is what the "boys" wanted, and they would have returned as heads of the expedition if the Columbus brothers had not been a little too much for them.

The celerity with which Columbus got away this time and the ample provision made for his fleet strongly suggest a desire to get rid of him on the part of Ferdinand and an uneasy conscience over his treatment, by Isabella. He asked for the fleet on February 26, 1502; the Sovereigns authorized it on March 14 and ordered him to make all convenient speed westward "since the present season is very good for navigation" (which of course it was not). He actually organized an expedition of four caravels in a little more than two weeks.

The Admiral's main object in this voyage was to find a strait between Cuba (which he still assumed to be China) and the continent that he discovered in 1498. Since that time Hojeda and Bastidas had pushed along the Spanish Main as far as the Gulf of Darien, but the shores and waters of the Caribbean west of a line drawn from Darien to Bahía Cortés, Cuba, including the entire Gulf of Mexico, were still unknown and unexplored by Europeans. Here, Columbus believed, was the key to the great geographical riddle, the relation of his recent discoveries to Asia. Here he expected to find the strait through which Marco Polo had sailed from China into the Indian Ocean. And the Sovereigns gave him a letter of introduction to Vasco da Gama, again outward bound around the Cape of Good Hope, in the hope that the two would meet somewhere in India. For nobody yet even suspected the existence of the Pacific Ocean; the Ocean was still all one, laving Europe and Africa in the west, Asia and Africa in the east. The Indian Ocean was a mere bay of it, like the Mediterranean, readily accessible through the expected strait in the western Caribbean.

The Admiral had hoped to be allowed to design and build some new small vessels embodying improvements that would make it possible to sail to windward even against a contrary current, but there was no time for that. He had to take what he could get, which was not too bad. Each of his four caravels was about the size of *Niña*, square-rigged with small main topsails. Columbus and his son sailed in the largest, the name of which we do not know; she was always called *La Capitana*, The Flagship; her burthen was 70 tons. Her captain was Diego Tristán, who had been with the Admiral on his Second Voyage, and she carried a crew of two officers, fourteen able seamen, twenty boys and seven petty officers, including two trumpeters, presumably to provide a dignified entry for the Admiral to Oriental courts. One of her interesting passengers was an Irish wolfhound which the Admiral brought along for anti-Indian warfare.

The second vessel of this fleet, called *La Gallega*, The Galician, was distinguished by a bonaventure mizzen, a tiny fourth mast stepped on the taffrail, like the jigger of a modern yawl. Pedro de Terreros, the only man who is known to have sailed on all four of Columbus's voyages, commanded *La Gallega*, and Juan Quintero, her owner, shipped as master. She carried a boatswain, nine able seamen, fourteen boys and one gentleman volunteer. Next in burthen was *Santiago de Palos*, nicknamed *Bermuda* after her owner and master Francisco Bermúdez. Her captain was Francisco Porras, whose brother Diego sailed with him as chief clerk and comptroller. Bartholomew Columbus sailed in *Bermuda* without office or pay but always took command in time of stress. She carried eleven able seamen and a boatswain, six gentlemen volunteers, twelve boys and four petty officers. Smallest of the fleet, measuring about 50 tons, was *Vizcaína*, the Biscayan, commanded by Bartolomeo Fieschi, scion of a leading Genoese family which had befriended the humble Colombos in times past. She carried eight able seamen, a boatswain, three gentlemen, ten boys and the fleet chaplain, Fray Alixandre.

All except the Columbus family were on the royal payroll; the captains got 4000 maravedis (about twenty-seven dollars in gold, or five and a half guineas) a month; the able seamen were paid one quarter of that, and the boys about one guinea, or a five-dollar gold piece. It does not sound very much, but everyone had six months' advance, and those who survived the voyage had a pot of money due to them on their return.

Comparing the crew list with that of the First Voyage, the only other complete one we have, the principal difference was the large number of boys between twelve and eighteen years old carried in the Fourth Voyage. The Admiral had evidently discovered that on a voyage of discovery and high adventure young fellows make better seamen and obey orders more briskly than old shellbacks who grouse and grumble and growl out of the corners of their mouths, "What's the idea? Old Captain so-and-so didn't do it that way," and declare that the new islands are not worth a ducat apiece, and hanker after the fleshpots of Marseilles, Naples and Lisbon.

The fleet sailed from Seville April 3, 1502, and on the way down-river careened at Casa de Viejo to clean the ships' bottoms and pay them with pitch to discourage teredos; but on this voyage the teredos ate right through the pitch and liked it. From the river mouth the caravels proceeded to Cadiz, where Columbus and his twelve-year-old son Ferdinand came on board. We are indebted to Ferdinand for the most detailed account of this High Voyage, in his biography of his father. He wrote it many years later, but his youthful impressions were still vivid, and although the Admiral said that Ferdinand qualified as able seaman in the course of it, he never wished to go to sea again.

At Cadiz the fleet was delayed by foul winds until May 11, when it sailed with a favoring northerly. After calling at Arzila on the coast of Morocco, it reached Las Palmas on May 20 and sailed from the Grand Canary on the twenty-fifth. "West and by South," the same course as the Second Voyage, was set by the Admiral. We have no details of the ocean passage, but it must have been uneventful, with continual fair wind, because it was completed in only twenty-one days. On June 15 they made landfall on Martinique, next island south of Dominica, tarried there three days for rest, refreshment and to wash clothes, apparently undisturbed by Amazons or Carib warriors, and then ranged the entire chain of Antilles discovered on the Second Voyage.

On June 29 the Admiral hove-to in the roadstead off Santo

Domingo. The Sovereigns had expressly forbidden him to visit his viceroyalty on the outward passage, lest he and Ovando run afoul of each other, but the Admiral had several good excuses, if not reasons, to look in at his own capital. He knew that Ovando was about to dispatch his grand fleet home and wished to send letters by it, and he hoped to persuade some shipmaster to swap a small, handy vessel for *Bermuda*, which had proved a dull sailer but would be good to carry cargo. Most important, he knew that a hurricane was making up and wished to take refuge. He had already experienced two hurricanes, one behind Saona in 1494 and another at Isabela in 1495, and recognized the portents only too well. An oily swell rolled in from the southeast, veiled cirrus clouds tore through the upper air, light gusty winds played over the surface of the water, low-pressure twinges were felt in his arthritic joints, and (a sign unknown to modern hydrographic offices) various denizens of the deep such as seal and manatee gamboled on the surface in large numbers. So, heaving-to off the Ozama River mouth, the Admiral sent ashore his senior captain, Pedro de Terreros, with a note to Governor Ovando, predicting a hurricane within two days, requesting permission to take refuge there, and begging the governor to keep all his ships in port and double their mooring lines. Ovando had the folly not only to disregard the request and warning, but to read the Admiral's note aloud with sarcastic comments to his heelers, who roared and rocked with laughter over this "soothsayer" who pretended to be able to predict the winds. And the great fleet proceeded to sea that very day, as the governor had planned.

It had just rounded into the Mona Passage, with the harborless southeastern coast of Hispaniola on the port hand, when the hurricane burst upon it from the northeast. Some ships foundered at sea, others which hove-to were driven onto the lee shore and destroyed; and among those that went down with all hands was

the flagship commanded by Antonio de Torres, carrying Bobadilla as passenger and a cargo estimated at over half a million dollars in gold. Nineteen ships sank with all hands, six others were
lost but left a few survivors, and four scudded safely around
Saona and into Santo Domingo, arriving in a sinking condition.
The only one that got through to Spain was the smallest, *Aguja*,
bearing Columbus's agent Carvajal with the Admiral's own gold,
which he had forced Bobadilla to disgorge.

Denied shelter for his fleet in the Ozama River, Columbus
sought it off the mouth of the Rio Jaina, a short distance west
of Santo Domingo. For he rightly guessed that the hurricane
would pass through the Mona Passage and along the north coast
of Hispaniola, so that the wind would blow off the southern
shore, which would afford the ships a lee. When night fell, the
north wind reached the height of its fury. Nobody then had any
means of measuring its force, but one hundred miles an hour
is normal in a West Indies hurricane, and there is no reason to
suppose that this one was soft; judging from Columbus's distance from the center, he could hardly have had it less than eighty
miles per hour. That is force 12 on the Beaufort scale in which,
according to Bowditch, "no canvas can stand." The three smaller
caravels parted their cables and were driven out to sea, but they
were well handled (*Bermuda* by Bartholomew Columbus, as
Captain Porras took to his bunk) and escaped with only superfi-
cial damage. The Admiral had every bit of ironmongery on
board frapped to *Capitana's* cables, and she rode it out. As he
remarked in a letter home, "What man ever born, not excepting
Job, would not have died of despair when in such weather, seeking safety for son, brother, shipmates and myself, we were forbidden the land and the harbor that I, by God's will and sweating blood, won for Spain!"

By God's will and a lot of sweating and swearing, all his ships came through, and, as agreed before the hurricane struck, all made rendezvous in Puerto Viejo de Azua, some fifty miles westward. Each feared that the others were lost, but, as if by a miracle, all caught the southeast breeze that followed the hurricane and scudded into that little landlocked harbor within a few hours of each other on Sunday, July 3. Columbus and his captains could not have done better if they had had storm warnings over the radio; even so, they might have done worse. One ship's boat and three anchors were the only serious losses.

After resting a week or ten days at Azua, Columbus put to sea again, steering southwest to the Alta Vela Channel, then west. Crossing the Windward Passage, the ships ran into a flat calm, and the men went ashore on Morant Cays to get fresh water. They then sailed along the south shore of Jamaica, thence northwest to a cay off the south coast of Cuba, probably Cayo Largo. On July 27 the wind turned northeast and the fleet weighed and crossed the Caribbean, 360 miles wide at this point, in three days. When the wind moderated, a lookout sighted the Bay Islands off the coast of Honduras.

At Bonacca, first of the Bay Islands where the fleet anchored, the Spaniards encountered the biggest native canoe any of them had seen: "long as a galley" and beamy, with a 'midships cabin for passengers and an interesting cargo of cotton cloth, copper implements and crucibles for smelting ore, with gourds full of beer made from the hubo fruit, and cacao beans which the Jicaque Indians of Honduras used, even recently, as currency. The canoe had come from the mainland and was trading with the islands. Columbus forcibly retained the skipper, whom he renamed Juan Pérez, as guide and interpreter.

From the Bay Islands it was only thirty miles to Cape Honduras, in the lee of which, off the site of the future city of Trujillo, the fleet anchored. And here began in earnest the Admiral's search

BAY ISLANDS
July 30
1502

Bonacca I.(Guanaca) *July 30*

Roatan I.

Puerto Castillo

C. Honduras (Pta Caxinas)

Aug. 14
(H.W.at Possession)

COSTA DE LAS OREJAS

M A I A

H O N D U R A S

85

15 ———— 15

C. Gracias á Dios, *Sept. 14*

Miskito Cays

Bragmans Bluff

COURSE OF COLUMBUS
ALONG HONDURAS, NICARAGUA
AND COSTA RICA ON HIS FOURTH
VOYAGE IN 1502

0   50   100 *Nautical miles*

0   100 *Kilometers*

Rio Grande

Rio de los Desastres? *Sept 16*

Tyra Cays (Quatros Tiempos)

N I C A R A G U A

Pearl Cays (Limones)

•Little Corn I.
○Great Corn I.

Bluefields Lagoon

Rio de los Desastres ?

LAGO DE NICARAGUA

Monkey Pt. Cabo de Rojas

San Juan del Norte

QUICURI CARIAI

C O S T A   R I C A

Pto Limon

Uva I. (La Huerta) ———— 10
Sept 25 - Oct 5

10

85

Raisz

for a strait. Should he turn west or east? West would be the easier going and the harder to get back from, and as Columbus had no knowledge of the Gulf of Mexico and knew that he was on about the same longitude as his farthest west in the "Chinese Province of Mangi" (Cuba), he figured that he was about half-way down the Malay Peninsula and that the Strait of Malacca lay south and east. So eastward he turned.

During a space of twenty-eight days, and from the Rio Romano to Cape Gracias à Dios, the fleet had a long and distressing beat to windward. "It was one continual rain, thunder and lightning," wrote Columbus. "The ships lay exposed to the weather, with sails torn, and anchors, rigging, cables, boats and many of the stores lost; the people exhausted and so down in the mouth that they were all the time making vows to be good, to go on pilgrimages and all that; yea, even hearing one another's confessions! Other tempests I have seen, but none that lasted so long or so grim as this. Many old hands whom we looked on as stout fellows lost their courage. What griped me most were the sufferings of my son; to think that so young a lad, only thirteen, should go through so much. But Our Lord lent him such courage that he even heartened the rest, and he worked as though he had been to sea all of a long life. That comforted me. I was sick and many times lay at death's door, but gave orders from a doghouse that the people clapped together for me on the poop deck. My brother was in the worst of the ships, the crank one, and I felt terribly having persuaded him to come against his will."

Nobody without Columbus's perseverance would have kept it up. The wind blew steadily from the east and the current ran counter to the course. Every morning the caravels had to heave up anchors and claw offshore on the starboard tack, often in heavy rain. At noon the fleet wore to the port tack, stood inshore again, and at sundown anchored off a sodden coast in an open roadstead, the caravels pitching and tossing all night, and the crew fighting mosquitoes from the swamps. Some days they gained a few miles; on others they fetched up opposite the same grove of obscene mangroves off which they had spent the previous night. The average distance made good was only six miles a day. But the Admiral had to be getting on; he dared not tarry for a fair wind, nor dared he stand well out to sea lest he miss the strait.

At last, on September 14, the fleet rounded a cape that the Admiral named Gracias à Dios, Thanks Be to God. It marked the end of his dead beat because the land here trended southward. Although the wind still blew from the east, they were able to jog along on the port tack a safe distance from shore. They anchored off Rio Grande, Nicaragua, to obtain wood and water; there two sailors were drowned crossing the bar, so the Admiral named the river Rio de los Desastres. They passed the site of San Juan del Norte and entered a region that the Indians called Cariai, the present Costa Rica.

Ten days were passed at anchor behind Uva Island, off the present Puerto Limón. Here they had friendly though somewhat aloof relations with the local Talamanca Indians. The usual rôles were reversed, the natives eager to do business and the Spaniards somewhat coy. First, the Indians swam out to the caravels with a line of cotton jumpers and ornaments of *guanin*, the gold and copper alloy that Columbus had found in Paria on the Third Voyage. Evidently *guanin* was regarded in Spain as a poor substitute for pure gold, and Columbus would have none of it, but gave the would-be traders some presents to take ashore. Next, to break down "sales resistance," the Indians sent on board two virgins, one about eight and the other about fourteen years old; "they showed great courage," recorded Ferdinand (who was then about the same age as the elder), "exhibited neither grief nor sorrow but always looked pleasant and modest; hence they were well treated by the Admiral, who caused them to be fed and clothed and sent them ashore." (Columbus, on the contrary, wrote that they behaved so immodestly that "more could not be expected from public women" — and he should have known.) In any case, the continence of the Spaniards astonished the natives, and when next day Bartholomew went ashore, attended by clerk Torres with paper, pen and inkhorn, to take formal possession, the Indians took this to be magical apparatus and tossed brown powder into the air as "good joss" to counteract these apparently sexless sorcerers from Spain.

To reconnoiter this part of Costa Rica, Columbus sent an armed party up country. They reported an abundance of game — deer, pumas and the turkeylike bird now called the pavón — and brought back a spider monkey which one of the crossbowmen had wounded as a pet. In the meantime the Indians at Puerto Limón had presented the Admiral with a pair of peccaries, one of which he kept; it was so fierce and aggressive that the Irish wolf-hound retreated below decks and stayed there as long as the wild pig was on board. Piggy met his match, however, in the spider monkey, which, wounded though it was, coiled its tail around the peccary's snout, seized him by the nape of the neck, and bit him until he roared with pain. This was thought to be wonderful sport, since kindness to animals was then no part of Christian mores.

On October 5 the search for the strait was renewed, and toward evening Columbus believed that he had found it in a channel, the Boca del Dragón, that leads into a great bay now named Almirante after him. Once inside, he found Indians wearing disks of fine gold on their breasts. For the standard price of three hawks' bells, value about a penny, the Spaniards were able to buy a gold disk worth a double eagle, or four guineas.

At this point the Spaniards were without an interpreter, as

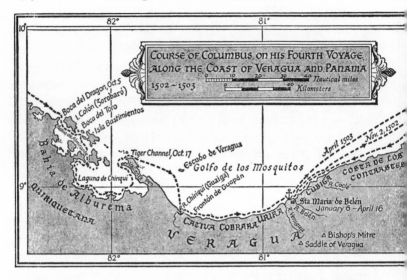

"Juan Pérez" had been allowed to go home. So, when Columbus asked for a strait to a wide ocean in sign language — extending his arms, pointing to salt water and describing a circle — the Indians waved him on by similar gestures to a narrow strait (now called Split Hill Channel) that led out of the lagoon. The caravels sailed through, although the channel was so narrow that their yards brushed the trees, and were rewarded by the sight of a great expanse of water. But, alas, there were mountains on every side; this was not the Indian Ocean but Chiriqui Lagoon.

For ten days the fleet idled about the shores of this lagoon, the Guaymi Indians plying a brisk trade in gold disks and bird-shaped amulets that they wore about their necks and which the Spaniards called eagles. From them Columbus learned that he was on an isthmus between two seas, but that a high cordillera barred his way. He also picked up from the Indians, or misunderstood them to say, that their neighbors on the other side of the cordillera

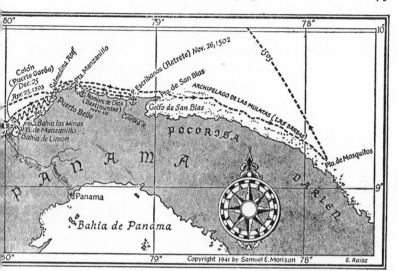

Copyright 1941 by Samuel E. Morison   E. Raisz

had warships complete with cannon, and that the Ganges River was only ten days' sail away. Referring to his Latin Bible, the Admiral inferred that this region, not Hispaniola, was the Ophir of 2 Chronicles viii 18, whence Hiram brought four hundred fifty talents of gold to Solomon. Apparently he also satisfied himself that there was no strait (nor was there), since from now on he appears to have concentrated on gathering gold and establishing a trading post. At least, there is no further mention of searching for a strait in any contemporary account of this voyage.

On October 17, 1502, a day of westerly wind, the fleet passed out of Chiriqui Lagoon by the eastward channel and sailed along harborless Mosquito Gulf, working its way east against the trade wind. These shores are superficially attractive but fundamentally inhospitable. From Chiriqui Lagoon to Limón Bay (the Caribbean entrance to the Panama Canal), a distance of over 125 miles, there are no harbors except where a river mouth has built up a bar over which only a canoe can enter if the bar is not breaking. Because of this, and because the Indians made menacing gestures at the few roadsteads where he anchored and sent a boat ashore, Columbus merely planted a mental buoy off the gold-bearing coast and pressed forward as fast as the rather exceptional west winds would take him, hoping to find a more hospitable spot for a trading post.

An unusually boisterous rainy season set in before the end of October. On November 2, after running before the wind, the four caravels entered a fine harbor which the Admiral named Puerto Bello, and it still is so called; during the Spanish colonial regime it was a thriving city at the northern end of the trans-isthmian mule track. If Columbus had decided to locate there, his garrison would certainly have heard of the Isthmus of Panama and obtained a glimpse of the Pacific Ocean ten years before Balboa did. But the Indians there, though friendly, had no gold, so the Admiral stayed a week, obtained provisions and cotton, and continued his voyage.

On November 9 the fleet made a little easting, but next day the wind forced them back several miles and they entered a harbor which Columbus named Puerto de Bastimentos, Harbor of Provisions. Ten years later Nicuesa renamed it Nombre de Dios and founded a town which long shared the transit trade with Puerto Bello and was duly sacked by Francis Drake. There the Columbus fleet remained twelve days, making minor repairs while the wind stayed in the east. And again the Admiral missed a chance to start a settlement at a proper site.

Their next stop was at a tiny harbor which they called El Puerto del Retrete, now called Escribanos. It was so small that the four caravels had to tie up alongside the banks as to a wharf. This gave the men a chance to sneak off to Indian villages and do some private trading with a gun, and that made trouble. A swarm of Indians gathered on the beach and made threatening gestures, and the Admiral had to mow down a few with gunfire before the rest would disperse.

Tired of sitting out the east wind, Columbus now decided to turn back to Veragua and take measures to obtain more of that gold. On December 5 the fleet returned to Puerto Bello. Next day the wind whipped around into the west again. For a month the caravels were batted back and forth between Puerto Bello and somewhere near the mouth of the Chagres River. The current always changed with the wind; it was no use trying to buck it. The weather was unusually foul. "I don't say it rained," recorded Columbus, "because it was like another deluge," with thunder and lightning whenever the wind changed. Once the fleet was threatened by a tremendous waterspout, but it passed harmlessly by after the Admiral had exorcised it by reading aloud from the Gospel according to Saint John the account of that famous tempest on the Sea of Galilee concluding, "Fear not, it is I." Then, clasping the Bible in his left hand, with drawn sword he traced a cross in the sky and a circle around the fleet. That night *Vizcaína* lost sight of her consorts but found them again after three very dark and tempestuous days. The people were so worn out, said the Admiral, that they longed for death to end their sufferings. Then came two days of calm, during which great schools of shark lashed around the caravels; many were taken and some eaten, as provisions were running low. Ferdinand remembered that the hardtack had become so full of weevils than some men waited for darkness to eat a porridge made of it, but others did not even trouble to wait, "because they might lose their supper had they been so nice."

On December 23 the fleet put in at the present harbor of Cristóbal, Panama Canal Zone, and there kept Christmas and New Year's, 1503, very miserably, riding at anchor off the site of the Coco Solo naval base. Here, had he only known it, Columbus was within a few miles of solving the riddle of the strait. He might have sent his boats up the Chagres, borrowed Indian canoes, and from the head of navigation he would have been only twelve miles by land from the Pacific Ocean. But he was so exhausted and humbled, and his men so beaten down by their long buffeting, that they had no energy left for exploration, and apparently they had little converse with the Indians of the future Canal Zone, or did not understand them. So Columbus missed by a few miles the most important geographical discovery that he could have made on the High Voyage.

CHAPTER XIX

Belén

RETURNING WESTWARD along the inhospitable coast of Veragua, Columbus searched for a likely place to found a trading post which would draw in the abundant gold of that region, and on January 6 anchored off the mouth of a river that he named Belén, Bethlehem, because it was the Feast of the Three Kings who brought gifts of gold, myrrh and frankincense to the infant Jesus. A good omen! Sounding from the boats, he found seven feet of water over the bar and towed his caravels inside where the river forms a basin with plenty of water. They were just in time, as next day another storm blew up, and any kind of sea on that coast breaks on the river bars.

The coastal plain here is very narrow, not more than a few yards wide in some places, and behind it rises rugged, broken country covered by impenetrable rain forest, and behind that, verdure-clad mountains whose summits are usually covered with clouds. The trade wind beats in on this coast, which consists of long sand beaches separated by rocky bluffs. It is dangerous to try to anchor and in most places impossible to land in small boats. Rainfall is so excessive that agriculture on any large scale is unprofitable. The few people who live along that shore today have no means of communication with the outside world except by dugout canoe; boats can be launched only when the sea is exceptionally calm. We, on the Harvard Columbus Expedition, found this the most difficult region of all those discovered by the Admiral to examine. Only through the coöperation of the Panama Government, which provided us with a diesel-powered trading sloop and a good native pilot, did we manage to effect a landing (after sundry tumblings in the surf) at the Rio Belén.

A few days after the Epiphany, Bartholomew Columbus took the ships' boats westward along the coast and rowed up the next river, the Veragua, toward the seat of a cacique named Quibián. Dignified but friendly, Quibián came downstream with a fleet of canoes to greet the visitors and next day was entertained by the Admiral on board *Capitana*.

Veragua has one of the heaviest rainfalls in the world, and the ground is so thoroughly soaked that every storm starts a freshet. Columbus experienced this on January 24, 1503. Following a rainstorm in the mountains, a torrent roared down on the caravels in the Belén mooring basin. *Capitana* dragged, fouled *Gallega* and carried away her bonaventure mizzen, and only by quick work were both vessels kept from broaching on the bar. Two weeks of rain and flood followed; it was not until February 6 that the sea was calm enough for the boats to get out. Bartholomew then made a return visit to Quibián and marched upcountry along an Indian trail with native guides. His men in one day, with no other implements but their knives, collected about ten dollars' worth of gold apiece. The discovery of this auriferous region so pleased the Admiral that he decided to build a fortified trading post at Belén, leave his brother in charge, and return to Spain for reinforcements. A little hill near the mouth of the river was chosen for the site, and the men began to construct the post, which Columbus named Santa María de Belén. He had chosen just about the worst spot on the coast of Central America to establish a beachhead.

In 1940, when we were ranging this coast to check up on Columbus, we encountered an old prospector who explained why

Veragua had never been properly exploited for gold. Years before, he went up one of the rivers with a partner and an Indian guide. "Where do we find gold?" he asked, after paddling many miles. "Right here!" said the Indian, who pulled out a clasp knife, dug some clay from the river bank and panned out some ten dollars' worth of shining gold grains! The prospector and his partner began at once to plan how to spend their first million dollars. They returned to the nearest town for supplies and lumber and built sluice boxes, the product of which should have made them rich. But in the next freshet all their gear was washed down into the Caribbean. That has happened again and again during the last four and a half centuries. There is still "gold in them thar hills," but only the Indians know how to get it out.

By the time that Santa María de Belén had become an incipient trading factory of a dozen palm-thatched houses, the river fell so low that the caravels could not cross the bar. And at this juncture, when they were fairly caught inside, there came the inevitable change of attitude on the part of the Guaymi Indians. Sailors had been sneaking off by twos and threes to trade with a gun and get women. Quibián could put up with a good deal of that if he believed that his importunate visitors would shortly depart, but now that it was evident they intended to build a town and settle, he decided it was time to give them "the treatment." He sent reconnoitering parties in canoes to Belén, who acted so suspiciously that Diego Méndez, a gentleman volunteer in the fleet, offered to row along the coast to learn what was going on. After a few miles he came upon a camp of a thousand howling warriors. Méndez, with that amazing nerve of the Spaniard in face of danger, stepped ashore alone to confront them; then, returning to his boat, kept just out of arrow range all night, observing the Indians' movements. They, apparently realizing that surprise had been lost, retreated to Quibián's village. Méndez, after reporting to the Admiral, followed them thither, and, in the midst of an ungodly up-roar, coolly pulled out a barber's kit and had his hair cut by his companion, Rodrigo de Escobar. This not only stopped the shout-ing but so interested Quibián that he had his hair trimmed, too, and was then presented with the shears, mirror and comb; and Méndez returned in peace.

Columbus should now have taken the hint that his trading post would be untenable in the face of the hostility of thousands of Indians who could sneak up under cover of the thick jungle and overwhelm it. Instead, he made a very bad decision — to seize Quibián and hold him as hostage for the Guaymís' good behavior. This was done promptly, under Diego Méndez's leadership. The cacique and about thirty members of his household were ambushed by an armed party of Spaniards and carried down-river, together with a big haul of gold objects. But Quibián escaped and promptly raised the country against the intruders.

In the meantime, seamen were towing three caravels over Belén bar, intending to leave *Gallega* behind as a floating fortress for the use of Bartholomew and the garrison. On April 6, while fare-wells were being said and only twenty men and the Irish wolf-hound were guarding the fort, it was attacked by about four hun-dred Indians armed with bows and arrows and spears. They were beaten off, largely through the rough work of the hound, but the Indians promptly got their revenge by killing Captain Diego Tristán of *Capitana*, who with a boat party was filling the flag-ship's water casks upstream. Only one Spaniard escaped from the boat and ten were killed.

The Admiral, who was ill with malaria, remained alone on board *Capitana* anchored outside the bar while all his men rowed ashore to help the garrison. He climbed to the main top and shouted to the men to return, but they could not hear his voice above the hideous whoops and screams of the Indians. He became delirious, saw visions and heard a voice which he believed to be that of God Almighty reminding him that he had done as much for Columbus as for Moses and David, that his tribulations were "written on tablets of marble," and that he was not to fear, "but have trust."

For eight days matters remained at an impasse. The weather was not too bad for the caravels outside, but no boat could get over the bar, and *Capitana* had to be given a skeleton crew from *Vizcaína* and *Bermuda*. In the meantime some of the Indian hostages on board *Bermuda* escaped, and those who did not, managed to hang themselves from the deck beams while confined in the hold.

The Admiral now made a hard but wise decision. Reflecting that, without hostages, Bartholomew's situation ashore must be desperate, he asked for a volunteer to swim across the bar and get into communication with his brother. Pedro de Ledesma volunteered. He returned with an urgent request from Bartholomew that he and the garrison abandon the fort and go home with the fleet. Columbus remembered the fate of the Navidad garrison and consented. Diego Méndez built a raft upon which all the Spaniards ashore, with most of their stores and gear, were lightered across the bar. *Gallega* was abandoned, along with Santa María de Belén. And no subsequent attempt to found a European settlement there or thereabouts ever succeeded. The descendants of the Guaymis have retreated to the interior, and, except for a few clearings where a handful of half-breeds live in poverty, the coast of Veragua is as wild and wet and forbiddingly beautiful as when Columbus landed there on the Feast of the Three Kings in 1503.

CHAPTER XX

Marooned in Jamaica

ON EASTER SUNDAY, April 16, 1503, *Capitana*, *Bermuda* and *Vizcaína* departed Belén roads, hoping by Whitsuntide to make Santo Domingo. There the Admiral proposed to call for repairs and provisions before returning home. Estimating that he was many leagues west of the meridian of Hispaniola, and knowing by experience that it was almost impossible to beat against the easterly trades and the equatorial current, he planned to edge along the coast of terra firma, working the land breeze and anchoring in bad weather, until he reached a point due south of Hispaniola, thence to fetch Santo Domingo on the starboard tack. This seamanlike decision caused discontent among the men because the pilots, wrong as usual, estimated that they were already due south of Santo Domingo, or even Puerto Rico.

Unfortunately, the three caravels were riddled with teredos. Columbus was blamed for this neglect, and it is not clear why he did not heave his fleet down either at Cayo Largo in Cuba or at Coco Solo, where he did careen *Gallega*, the one left behind. He answered this and other criticisms in his report to the Sovereigns, thus:

Let those who are fond of blaming and finding fault, while they sit safely at home, ask, "Why did you not do thus and so?" I wish they were on this voyage; I well believe that another voyage of a different kind awaits them, or our faith is naught!

In other words, to hell with armchair admirals and library navigators!

As the voyage alongshore progressed, all hands were kept busy at the pumps or bailing with kettles. Nevertheless, *Vizcaína* had to be abandoned in a hopelessly leaky condition at Puerto Bello, and her crew divided between *Capitana* and *Bermuda*. They crawled along, past their former farthest east in the present Republic of Panama, into the Gulf of San Blas. All hands were too busy trying to keep afloat to admire the scenery of this coast, the jagged cordillera rising from behind gleaming white beaches and the magnificent tropical rain forest of mahogany, ebony and other valuable woods, above whose glossy-leaved canopy an occasional giant of the forest thrusts a top bursting with pink or orange blossoms, as though a torch were being held up from the dark jungle.

On May 1 the two caravels reached a headland that Columbus named Cabo Marmóreo, the Marble Cape, probably the present Punta de Mosquitos. As the coast here began to trend southeastward into the Gulf of Darien, the pilots and captains, hopefully but wildly figuring that they were already east of the meridian of Guadeloupe, ganged up on Columbus and practically forced him to leave the coast and strike northward. Actually they were on the meridian of Kingston, Jamaica, and about 900 miles west of Guadeloupe. The Admiral wanted to sail alongshore as far east as Cabo de Vela before crossing, but nobody on board knew that coast, and he was so beaten down by arthritis, malaria and the failure of his plans that he gave in.

So, on May Day, 1503, worm-eaten *Capitana* and riddled *Bermuda* stood northward, sailing as close to the wind as they could, constantly set to leeward by the current. Ten days later they passed the Little Cayman northwest of Jamaica, and on the twelfth made a most unwelcome landfall on the Cuban archipelago which

Columbus had named the Queen's Garden on his Second Voyage. "Full of hunger and trouble," as Ferdinand records, the caravels dropped anchor in a little harbor with poor holding ground at Cay Breton. The people had "nothing to eat but hardtack and a little oil and vinegar, exhausted by working three pumps day and night because the vessels were ready to sink from the multitude of worms that had bored into them." On top of that, one of the night thunderstorms for which this coast is notorious burst upon them, causing *Bermuda* to part her cable and foul *Capitana*. The flagship passed her a line and *Capitana's* one remaining anchor — one for two vessels — fortunately held.

After six days the wind moderated and the caravels, with planking "like a honeycomb," as Ferdinand said, and the sailors "spiritless and desperate," continued to struggle east along the Cuban coast. By about June 10, when they were still west of Santiago, Columbus decided that the only way to save his people's lives was to stand out to sea on the port tack, hoping for a favorable slant that would take them across the Windward Passage to Cape Tiburon, Hispaniola. He later admitted that this was a mistake, that he should have made best speed, with sheets started, to Jamaica. For, when the caravels had reached a point estimated to be about a hundred miles from Hispaniola, the water gained on *Bermuda* at so alarming a rate that the Admiral ordered both caravels to square away for Jamaica. He might have taken *Bermuda's* crew on board *Capitana* and tried to make Hispaniola with her, but the flagship too was leaky, and he had no assurance that she was still capable of bucking a head wind for another hundred miles. And, since wooden ships labor much less with the wind aft, and sail faster, his decision to seek refuge at Jamaica was sound.

On June 25 the wretched vessels, their decks almost awash, entered St. Ann's Bay, Jamaica, which Columbus had named Santa Gloria on the Second Voyage. He ran them aground side by side on a sand beach and shored them up to keep on an even keel. High tides rose almost to their decks, upon which palm-thatched cabins had to be built for the people. And there they stayed for a year.

These 116 Spaniards marooned on Jamaica were fairly well situated for defense; the ships' hulks made a dry home and no mean fortress. A large and friendly Indian village lay nearby. Columbus, who knew by bitter experience that the natives would not long remain friendly if his people were allowed to make contact with them, ordered all hands to stay on board, and allowed nobody to go ashore without his permission.

The first thing that needed attention was the food supply. Columbus sent Diego Méndez and three men on a foraging expedition. They traveled almost to the east end of the island, purchased a dugout canoe, loaded it with native provisions, and returned to Santa Gloria in triumph; and, to insure a continuing supply, Méndez drew up a tariff agreement with the neighboring Indians to sell a cake of cassava bread for two glass beads, two of the big rodents called hutía for a lace point, and a great quantity of anything, such as fish or maize, for a hawk's bell. Why these Spaniards and Genoese could not fish for themselves or plant their own cornfields has never been explained; it is clear that if the Indians had not fed them, they would have starved to death.

But how to get home? The final resting place of the two caravels commanded a wide sea view, but the chance of any Spanish or other vessel coming within sight was infinitesimal, for Columbus had let it be known that there was no gold in Jamaica. *Capitana* and *Bermuda* were beyond repair, and their crews appear to have been as incapable of building a small vessel to escape, as they were of feeding themselves. So the only possible way to avoid spending the rest of their lives in Jamaica was to send a messenger to Hispaniola, there to procure a rescue ship.

As usual, everyone said, "Let Diego Méndez do it!" That faithful and indefatigable Spaniard hauled out the big dugout canoe he had purchased, fixed a false keel and washboards, and fitted a mast and sail. On his first attempt he was captured by Indians somewhere near Northeast Point, escaped, and returned to Santa Gloria. On the next he had plenty of assistance. Bartolomeo Fieschi, the Genoese captain, undertook to pilot another canoe with him to Hispaniola, and Bartholomew Columbus provided an armed escort in the shape of a fleet of dugouts to protect Méndez and Fieschi in Jamaican waters. At or near Northeast Point farewells were exchanged, and the two canoes pushed out into the Windward Passage.

More to-do was made about this canoe trip than about anything else on the High Voyage. In comparison with numerous lifeboat and raft voyages in World War II, it does not seem a particularly long or difficult passage — only 108 miles from island to island, with a break at Navassa, 78 miles out; and the month was July, when the trades die down and before hurricanes blow up. But neither the Spaniards nor these Indians were used to small-boat journeys, and they certainly took this one hard. Each captain had a crew of six Christians and ten Indians, who were supposed to do the work. They started in a flat calm, which was what they wanted, and on the first day out were troubled only by the heat. The night was cool, but next morning it was discovered that the Indians had drunk up all their water rations. By the second sunset everyone was discouraged; one Indian died of thirst and others were too weak to paddle. And a third night fell with no sight of land. But when the moon rose, Diego Méndez observed the outline of Navassa Island against its lower limb. They reached the island in about seventy-two hours from Jamaica, having made a little better than a mile an hour. On Navassa everyone drank his fill of fresh water (some of the Indians dying of it), and they kindled a fire and cooked shellfish. Now they could see the lofty mountains of Hispaniola, and the following evening they made Cape Tiburon.

Fieschi wished to return to Jamaica to tell the Admiral that they had made it, but his crew refused. Diego Méndez obtained some fresh Indian paddlers, continued along the coast to Azua (where they had rendezvoused after the 1502 hurricane), and thence marched inland to meet Ovando and request that the Admiral be succored. It was now August 1503. The governor, who was enjoying his own rule in Hispaniola and feared lest Columbus be restored to office, was perfectly willing to let him spend the rest of his life in Jamaica. He kept Méndez in the interior, putting him off with promises for seven months. Finally in March 1504, he was allowed to go on foot to Santo Domingo and try to charter a vessel. Ovando had a station ship or two at Santo Domingo but refused to send one to rescue the Admiral.

Columbus and his men had no means of knowing whether their messengers had arrived or had perished. After six months had elapsed, and the winter northers made their position on the grounded ships very uncomfortable, a mutiny formed around the Porras brothers, the political appointees. They spread the word that Columbus was serving out a term of banishment and had no desire or intention to go to Santo Domingo. So, me lads, if you want to get out of this hell hole and back to Spain, join us; we'll grab a few guns, impress some Indian paddlers and get ourselves to Hispaniola. Let that cursed Genoese and his infatuated followers stay here and rot!

Forty-eight men, about half the total, began the mutiny on the day after New Year's, 1504. Crying the watchword "To Castile! To Castile!" the mutineers piled into ten dugout canoes and started eastward along the coast, robbing the Indians wherever they called. They had made only about fifteen miles from Northeast Point when a freshening breeze from the east forced them to put back. All their plunder had to be thrown overboard, and most of the Indian paddlers too. Two more attempts were made to cross, but both failed. So the Porras party abandoned their canoes and trudged back to Santa Gloria, living off the country.

Columbus's loyal men, in the meantime, were becoming very hungry. The Indians had few surplus stocks of food, and "consumer demand" for beads, lace points and hawks' bells had been exhausted. Moreover, said Ferdinand, the food consumption of one Spaniard was about equal to that of twenty Indians. At this critical juncture the Admiral pulled his famous eclipse trick. He had an almanac which predicted a total eclipse of the moon on the last night of February, 1504. So that day he summoned the nearby caciques and chief men on board stranded *Capitana*, told them that God desired the Indians to supply the Christians with food and would presently give them a clear token from Heaven of His displeasure at their failure to do so. They had better watch the moon that night. The eclipse began at moonrise, and as the black-out area increased, the Indians flocked to the ships, howling and lamenting, praying the Admiral to stop it. Columbus retired to his cabin while the eclipse lasted, emerged when he was certain from the almanac that the total phase was about over, and announced that he had interceded with the Almighty and promised in their name that they would provide the food the Christians wanted, in return for which God had consented to take the shadow away. It worked perfectly, and there was no more food shortage.

At the end of March, 1504, over eight months had elapsed since the canoe messengers had left for Hispaniola, and nothing had been heard of or from them. Suddenly a small caravel sailed in to Santa Gloria and anchored near the Spanish camp. This was the first sail the men had seen in two years. It had been sent by

Ovando to ascertain whether Columbus was still alive and report what he was doing. The governor was mean enough to order the captain, Diego de Escobar, not to take anyone home. But she did bring a welcome message from Méndez that he was doing his best to charter a rescue ship, and left a small gift from Ovando — two casks of wine and a side of salt pork.

When this caravel disappeared over the horizon, the morale of Columbus's men reached an all-time low. At the same time Columbus made advances to the Porras party, knowing that he would be blamed if that precious pair of brothers did not get home. The Porrases rejected his offers (which included a big slice of the salt pork), in the hope of suborning the Admiral's men and seizing the houseboats. They marched on Santa Gloria. The Columbus brothers mustered loyal men to meet them. A pitched battle, fought largely with swords for want of gunpowder, took place on May 29, and the loyalists won. The mutineers surrendered, all except the Porras brothers were pardoned, and they were allowed to stay on shore under guard.

Rescue was not long coming. Diego Méndez finally managed to charter a little caravel in Santo Domingo and sent her to Jamaica under command of Diego de Salcedo, a loyal servant of the Admiral. He made Santa Gloria in the latter part of June, 1504, took everyone on board, and on the twenty-ninth departed for Hispaniola. The survivors of the Fourth Voyage, about a hundred strong, had been in Jamaica a year and five days. The little caravel was in poor condition with a sprung mainmast, rotten sails and a foul bottom; she leaked so badly that they feared she would founder, and it took her six and a half weeks to reach Santo Domingo. There Columbus chartered another vessel and embarked for Spain on September 12 with his brother, Ferdinand, and twenty-two others of his company. A majority of the Fourth Voyage survivors elected to remain in Santo Domingo rather than risk another ocean passage. They had had enough work at the pumps to last ten lives!

The Admiral's homeward passage in the chartered ship was long and tempestuous; the foremast was sprung and the mainmast broke, but the Columbus brothers contrived a jury mast out of a spare yard. They did not reach Sanlúcar de Barrameda until November 7, 1504, a passage of fifty-six days.

So the High Voyage was over, after two and a half years at sea, including a year marooned in Jamaica. The most adventurous of the Admiral's four voyages, it was also the most disappointing. He had not discovered the strait, since none there was; the isthmus that he reported was of no interest to the Sovereigns, and the gold-bearing Veragua that he discovered was unexploitable. But he had done his best. As he wrote to son Diego shortly after his arrival:

I have served their Highnesses with as great diligence and love as I might have employed to win paradise and more; and if in somewhat I have been wanting, that was impossible, or much beyond my knowledge and strength. Our Lord God in such cases asketh nothing more of men than good will.

CHAPTER XXI

Home to Die

U PON HIS ARRIVAL in Spain after this long and distressing voyage, Columbus expected at the very least to be summoned to court to tell his story, a favor accorded to almost every captain of an overseas voyage, however insignificant. But the report he had sent home by Diego Méndez did not make a good impression. This *Lettera Rarissima*, as it is called, is rambling and incoherent. It contains some interesting information about what was to become the Spanish Main, together with too much self-justification and too many unconvincing "proofs" that he had been sailing along the Malay Peninsula, or somewhere in the Far East. By the time the Admiral reached Seville on November 8 or 9, 1504, the court was at Segovia and the Queen was confined to her bed with an illness that turned out to be her last. That was the excuse for not inviting the Admiral to court, but it was hardly convincing, since Isabella, even on her deathbed, was surrounded by weeping courtiers. And the splendid golden disks and "eagles" that Columbus brought from Veragua might have given her a little much-needed amusement. Probably it was King Ferdinand who, told that the troublesome Admiral was home again after everyone assumed he had been lost, gave orders that he must not be allowed to come to court and pester him with another tale of woe.

Isabella the Catholic died at Medina del Campo on November 26, 1504, greatly to Columbus's grief and loss. She had never sneered at him, she had understood what he was trying to do, she had respected his rights and protected him from the envious and the detractors. But the King had always considered the Admiral a bore, although he had supported him to please the Queen, and he was not interested in the New World, only in European wars and diplomacy. It would have been politic for Columbus to appear at the royal funeral, but arthritis had crept up on him and he was too ill to travel. Actually, there would have been no use in his making the tiring journey. Ferdinand was satisfied with Ovando's performance in Hispaniola, and the Admiral had a faithful advocate at court in the person of his son Don Diego, now about twenty-four years old and a member of the royal bodyguard. The younger son, Ferdinand, went back to his job as page and was given back pay for the Fourth Voyage as well. He had a wonderful tale of adventure to relate, but we gather that the courtiers were not interested in tempests and fights with Indians, and that, as a boy of sixteen who had seen the New World, he was a misfit at court.

Columbus was now living in a hired house in the parish of Santa María, Seville. He was not badly off, so far as this world's goods are concerned. His share of the gold obtained on the Fourth Voyage was considerable, and Carvajal had brought home a substantial sum for him in the *Aguja,* which survived the hurricane of 1502. We have a record of his selling part of it to goldsmiths for the equivalent of 660 guineas, or 165 double eagles. In addition, Ovando delivered to him at Santo Domingo in 1504 a chest of gold to take home, and he claimed about $180,000 more, still at Hispaniola, with his mark on it. But Columbus felt that he had been defrauded, and monotonously besought his son to obtain confirmation of what he called his "tithes," "eighths" and "thirds." The "tithe" was the ten per cent of the net exports from all lands that he discovered, guaranteed by the original contract of 1492. Columbus complained that the government allowed him only a tenth of their fifth of the gold; that is, two instead of ten per cent. The "eighth," similarly guaranteed, meant the profits on the Admiral's investments in one eighth of the cargo of any vessel trading with "The Indies." He had exercised this option in certain cargoes, but claimed that Bobadilla or Ovando had impounded his share and failed to pay up. The "third" was really a preposterous claim. Columbus's grant of the new office of Admiral of the Ocean Sea stated that it carried "pre-eminences and prerogatives . . . in the same manner as . . . the Grand Admiral of Castile." Having ascertained that the Grand Admiral collected a thirty-three and one third per cent tax on overseas trade within his jurisdiction — between Spain and the Canary Islands — Columbus claimed it as his due for the entire inward and outward trade of the Indies. Obviously, if that had been admitted, there would have been little profit left in American trade for anyone else, and he and his descendants would have become wealthier than the King of Spain or any other prince. As it was, even by collecting a mere two per cent of the gold, he was a rich man according to the standards of the day, and left substantial amounts to his sons.

It should be said that Columbus never intended to keep all this money. Even on his deathbed he was planning to accumulate a fund to finance a new crusade, and so provided in his last will and testament. It was always on his mind that the profits of his "Other World" might be used to recover the Holy Sepulchre from the infidel. And he was much more hurt over the slights to his dignity and honor than by the denial of what he deemed to be his property rights.

Even more was the Admiral concerned over collecting pay for the seamen and officers who had returned with him or in the Porras caravel. They now had two full years' wages due, and most of them were poor men with no other means of support. Thrice the Admiral begged the treasurer of Castile to pay them off, without result. Several of his loyal seamen were given jobs around Columbus's house. They even sent a delegation to court to ask for their back pay, with letters from the Admiral to his son and to persons of influence; but years elapsed before they received it.

By the first of 1505, Columbus came to the conclusion that it was useless to expect King Ferdinand to send him back to Hispaniola as Viceroy and Governor. In fact, the state of his health and his "advanced age" of fifty-three would have made another transatlantic voyage too risky. So he concentrated on trying to persuade the King to confer the viceroyalty on his son. Diego was then only twenty-five years old and had had no experience outside the court, but he was a clever courtier and made himself solid with the King by marrying a lady of royal blood, Doña María de Toledo. Three years after Columbus's death, Don Diego was appointed governor of Hispaniola and succeeded to his father's hereditary titles.

By the spring, Columbus felt well enough to travel, provided he could ride a mule; a horse's gait was too rough for him. The Spanish Government, under pressure by the horse breeders of Andalusia, had forbidden the use of mules for riding, so the Admiral had to petition the King for a special permit. That the King granted, the only favor he ever showed to Columbus. So, in May 1505, the Admiral started on his long journey to court, then at Segovia, north of Madrid.

King Ferdinand received him graciously and proposed that an arbitrator be appointed to settle his claims against the Crown. Columbus refused, because the King insisted that his viceroyalty and admiralty be adjudicated as well as the pecuniary claims, and he was too proud to arbitrate anything to which he had a clear legal title. The King then hinted that if Columbus would renounce all titles and offices, with the revenues pertaining to them, he would be granted a handsome estate with a fat rent roll. Columbus rejected that, absolutely. He considered it a dishonorable proposal. He would have all or nothing, and it was nothing that he got.

As the court moved to Salamanca and then to Valladolid, Columbus painfully followed. A year passed, nothing was accomplished, and in the meantime his arthritis grew worse. A large part of the time he was confined to bed in a hired house. But he felt so certain of justice being done that he made a will providing all sorts of legacies out of his rightful revenues, such as a sinking fund for the crusade, a house in Genoa to be kept open perpetually for his descendants, a chapel in Hispaniola endowed so that daily masses might be said for his soul forever. In his simplicity he seemed to feel that these pious bequests would attract the attention of the Almighty, who would see to it that the King made them practicable.

Almost at the last moment of his life, Columbus had his hopes raised by the arrival of the Infanta Juana in Spain to claim her mother's throne of Castile. She had been at court when Columbus first returned from the Indies, and he hoped that the favors granted by her sainted mother would be confirmed by her. He was too ill to move, so he sent brother Bartholomew to kiss the young Sovereign's hand and bespeak her favor.

While Bartholomew was absent on this mission, the Admiral began to sink. On May 19, 1506, he ratified his final will, creating Don Diego his principal heir and commending all other relatives, including his former mistress Beatriz, to his son's benevolence. Next day he suddenly grew worse. Both sons, the younger brother Diego and a few faithful followers such as Diego Méndez and Bartolomeo Fieschi gathered around his bedside. A priest was summoned, Mass was said, and everyone in the devoted circle of relatives, friends and domestics received the sacrament. After the concluding prayer, the Admiral, remembering the last words of his Lord and Saviour, murmured as his own, *In manus tuas, Domine, commendo spiritum meum* — "Into Thy hands, O Lord, I commit my spirit."

It was a poor enough deathbed for the Admiral of the Ocean Sea, Viceroy and Governor of the Islands and Mainlands in the Indies; and a poor enough funeral followed. No bishops or great dignitaries were present, and the official court chronicle mentioned neither death nor funeral. Columbus had the ill fortune to die at the moment when his discoveries were little valued, and his personal fortunes and expectations were at their lowest ebb.

Little by little, as his life receded into history and the claims of others to be the "real" discoverers of America faded into the background, his great achievements began to be appreciated. Yet it is one of the ironies of history that the Admiral himself died ignorant of what he had really accomplished, still insisting that he had discovered a large number of islands, a province of China and an "Other World"; but of the vast extent of that Other World, or of the ocean that lay between it and Asia, he had no knowledge.

Now, more than five hundred years after his birth, when the day that Columbus first raised an island in the New World is celebrated throughout the length and breadth of the Americas, his fame and reputation may be considered secure for all time. He had his faults and his defects, but they were largely the defects of the qualities that made him great — his indomitable will, his superb faith in God and in his own mission as the Christ-bearer to lands beyond the seas, his stubborn persistence despite neglect, poverty and discouragement. But there was no flaw, no dark side to the most outstanding and essential of all his qualities — his seamanship. As a master mariner and navigator, Columbus was supreme in his generation. Never was a title more justly bestowed than the one which he most jealously guarded — *Almirante del Mar Océano*, Admiral of the Ocean Sea.

Appendix

Columbus's Letter on His First Voyage

THIS IS A TRANSLATION, and the only one to be published since 1893, of the only surviving copy of the first edition of Columbus's Letter on his First Voyage, now one of the treasures of the New York Public Library. The original is a four-page black-letter folio, with neither title nor colophon. All bibliographers agree that it is the first edition and that it was printed in Barcelona, probably in mid-April 1493, directly from Columbus's manuscript. The manuscript is dated February 15 on board *Niña*, and was forwarded from Lisbon March 14, 1493. For text I have used the facsimile published by Quaritch of London in 1891 as *The Spanish Letter of Columbus*. There is a less clear facsimile in John Boyd Thacher, *Christopher Columbus, his Life, his Work, his Remains* (1903), II, 17–20. I have made a fresh translation of it, since all those made hitherto, that I have seen, except Quaritch's, were made from the synthetic text that a classical scholar concocted out of the several editions.

Before the end of April, 1493, the Letter was translated into Latin by one Cosco at Rome and there printed in May, and this Latin translation ran through at least seventeen editions during the years 1493–1499. Cosco misunderstood some of the original, which he tried to improve at certain points, yet almost all existing versions of the Letter are translations of the Latin translation. There is no evidence in Columbus's other letters, which are fairly numerous for that era, that he took the trouble to correct the many misprints, some of which are indicated in the notes to my translation.

The Letter is usually called "Columbus's Letter to Santangel," since the first edition was addressed to that crown official, or to "Gabriel" or "Raphael" Sanchez or Sanxis, treasurer of the Kingdom of Aragon, to whom the Latin translation says it was addressed. Actually it is Columbus's official report on his First Voyage to Ferdinand and Isabella, transmitted to them with a covering letter, long since lost. Probably it was then considered disrespectful in Spain to address such a report to the King or Queen unless one were a grandee or royal official; at any rate, Columbus always sent his important reports to a friend at court, ⁻vho was supposed to transmit or read them to the Sovereigns at the proper moment. It was natural that he should have addressed this Letter to Santangel, since he was the official who helped the Queen to make up her mind and who had found the money for the voyage. Possibly the other copy, which Columbus sent from Seville, was addressed to Gabriel Sanchez, or else the Latin translator assumed that Sanchez, not Santangel, was the Escribano de Ración (Keeper of the Privy Purse) referred to as the recipient of the Letter.

The New York Public Library also has a copy of the first illustrated Latin edition (Basle, 1493). The illustrations, including an ocean-going ship and an alleged Landing of Columbus (from a forty-oared Mediterranean galley!), had all been used in earlier works printed in Switzerland and really have nothing to do with the First Voyage. A facsimile of this edition has been printed by that library, with translation. The Clements Library at Ann Arbor, Michigan, has a copy of the first Latin edition, which it reprinted in facsimile, with translation, in 1952.

The Columbus Letter is not only the first of all *Americana;* it is a vital document for the Admiral himself, relating what he wished important people to think about his discovery, appealing alike to their piety and their cupidity, and concealing matters that he did not care to be broadcast, such as the near mutiny of his men, the loss of his flagship, and the disloyalty of Martín Alonso Pinzón.

Proper names that are reproduced just as they are spelled in the original, are italicized. I have supplied punctuation, which is almost wholly wanting in the original, and the paragraphing, too, is mine.

LETTER OF COLUMBUS

SIR, since I know that you will take pleasure at the great victory with which Our Lord has crowned my voyage, I write this to you, from which you will learn how in twenty [1] days I reached the Indies with the fleet which the most illustrious King and Queen, our lords, gave to me. And there I found very many islands filled with people without number, and of them all I have taken possession for their Highnesses, by proclamation and with the royal standard displayed, and nobody objected. To the first island which I found I gave the name *Sant Salvador*, in remembrance of His Heavenly Majesty, who marvelously hath given all this; the Indians call it *Guanahani*. To the second I gave the name *Isla de Santa Maria de Concepción;* to the third, *Ferrandina;* to the fourth, *La Isla Bella;* [2] to the fifth, *La Isla Juana;* and so to each one I gave a new name.

When I reached Juana, I followed its coast to the westward, and I found it to be so long that I thought it must be the mainland, the province of Catayo. [3] And since there were neither towns nor cities on the coast, but only small villages, with the people of which I could not have speech because they all fled forthwith, I went forward on the same course, thinking that I should not fail to find great cities and towns. And, at the end of many leagues, seeing that there was no change and that the coast was bearing me to the north, which was contrary to my desire since winter was already beginning and I proposed to go thence to the south, and as moreover the wind was favorable, I determined not to wait for a change of weather and backtracked to a notable harbor; [4] and thence I sent two men upcountry to learn if there were a king or great cities. They traveled for three days and found an infinite number of small villages and people without number, but nothing of importance; hence they returned.

I understood sufficiently from other Indians, whom I had al-

[1] *Veinte.* Probably a misprint for *treinte*, or xxxiii. The actual time, as we have seen, was thirty-three days. All other numerals in the original text are Roman.

[2] Misprint for *Isabela*, the name he gave to Crooked Island. Conception was Rum Cay; Ferrandina, Long Island; and Juana, Cuba.

[3] Meaning, a province of China.

[4] Puerto Gibara.

ready taken, that continually [5] this land was an island, and so I followed its coast eastwards 107 leagues up to where it ended. And from that cape I saw toward the east another island, distant 18 leagues from the former, to which I at once gave the name *La Spañola*. And I went there and followed its northern part, as I had in the case of Juana, to the eastward for 178 great leagues in a straight line. As Juana, so all the others are very fertile [6] to an excessive degree, and this one especially. In it there are many harbors on the coast of the sea, incomparable to others which I know in Christendom, and numerous rivers, good and large, which is marvelous. Its lands are lofty and in it there are very many sierras and very high mountains, to which the island *Centrefrei* [7] is not comparable. All are most beautiful, of a thousand shapes, and all accessible and filled with trees of a thousand kinds and tall, and they seem to touch the sky; and I am told that they never lose their foliage, which I can believe, for I saw them as green and beautiful as they are in Spain in May, and some of them were flowering, some with fruit, and some in another condition, according to their quality. And there were singing the nightingale and other little birds of a thousand kinds in the month of November, there where I went. There are palm trees of six or eight kinds, which are a wonder to behold on account of their beautiful variety, and so are the other trees and fruits and herbs; therein are marvelous pine groves, and extensive champaign country; and there is honey, and there are many kinds of birds and a great variety of fruits. Upcountry there are many mines of metals, and the population is innumerable. *La Spañola* is marvelous, the sierras and the mountains and the plains and the champaigns and the lands are so beautiful and fat for planting and sowing, and for livestock of every sort, and for building towns and cities. The harbors of the sea here are such as you could not believe in without seeing them, and so the rivers, many and great, and good streams, the most of which bear gold. And the trees and fruits and plants have great differences from

[5] *Continuamente*. Not clear whether he meant that the Indians told him continually that Cuba was an island, or what.

[6] *Fortissimas*. Probably a printer's error for *fertilissimas*.

[7] An obvious misprint for Tenerife.

those of La Juana; in this there are many spices and great mines of gold and of other metals.

The people of this island and of all the other islands which I have found and seen, or have not seen, all go naked, men and women, as their mothers bore them, except that some women cover one place only with the leaf of a plant or with a net of cotton which they make for that. They have no iron or steel or weapons, nor are they capable of using them, although they are well-built people of handsome stature, because they are wonderfully timorous. They have no other arms than arms of canes, [cut] when they are in seed time, to the ends of which they fix a sharp little stick; and they dare not make use of these, for oftentimes it has happened that I have sent ashore two or three men to some town to have speech, and people without number have come out to them, and as soon as they saw them coming, they fled; even a father would not stay for his son; and this not because wrong has been done to anyone; on the contrary, at every point where I have been and have been able to have speech, I have given them of all that I had, such as cloth and many other things, without receiving anything for it; but they are like that, timid beyond cure. It is true that after they have been reassured and have lost this fear, they are so artless and so free with all they possess, that no one would believe it without having seen it. Of anything they have, if you ask them for it, they never say no; rather they invite the person to share it, and show as much love as if they were giving their hearts; and whether the thing be of value or of small price, at once they are content with whatever little thing of whatever kind may be given to them. I forbade that they should be given things so worthless as pieces of broken crockery and broken glass, and ends of straps, although when they were able to get them, they thought they had the best jewel in the world; thus it was ascertained that a sailor for a strap received gold to the weight of two and a half *castellanos*,[8] and others much more for other things which were worth much less; yea, for new *blancas*,[9] for them they would give all that they

---

[8] $7.50, or a guinea and a half in gold.
[9] A copper coin worth half a maravedi, about a third of a cent.

had, although it might be two or three castellanos' weight of gold or an *arrova* [10] or two of spun cotton; they even took pieces of the broken hoops of the wine casks and, like animals, gave what they had, so that it seemed to me to be wrong and I forbade it, and I gave them a thousand good, pleasing things which I had brought, in order that they might be fond of us, and furthermore might be made Christians and be inclined to the love and service of their Highnesses and of the whole Castilian nation, and try to help us and to give us of the things which they have in abundance and which are necessary to us. And they know neither sect nor idolatry, with the exception that all believe that the source of all power and goodness is in the sky, and they believe very firmly that I, with these ships and people, came from the sky, and in this belief they everywhere received me, after they had overcome their fear. And this does not result from their being ignorant, for they are of a very keen intelligence and men who navigate all those seas, so that it is marvelous the good account they give of everything, but because they have never seen people clothed or ships like ours.

And as soon as I arrived in the Indies, in the first island which I found, I took by force some of them in order that they might learn [Castilian] and give me information of what they had in those parts; it so worked out that they soon understood us, and we them, either by speech or signs, and they have been very serviceable. I still have them with me, and they are still of the opinion that I come from the sky, in spite of all the intercourse which they have had with me, and they were the first to announce this wherever I went, and the others went running from house to house and to the neighboring towns with loud cries of, "Come! Come! See the people from the sky!" Then all came, men and women, as soon as they had confidence in us, so that not one, big or little, remained behind, and all brought something to eat and drink, which they gave with marvelous love. In all the islands they have very many *canoas* like rowing *fustes,* some bigger and some smaller, and some are bigger than a *fusta* [11] of eighteen benches.

[10] A weight equivalent to 25 lbs., or 11½ kilos.

[11] A long, light boat propelled chiefly by oars, common in the Mediterranean.

They are not so broad, because they are made of a single log, but a *fusta* could not keep up with them by rowing, since they make incredible speed, and in these [canoes] they navigate all those islands, which are innumerable, and carry their merchandise. Some of these canoes I have seen with 70 and 80 men in them, each one with his oar.

In all these islands, I saw no great diversity in the appearance of the people or in their manners and language, but they all understand one another, which is a very singular thing, on account of which I hope that their Highnesses will determine upon their conversion to our holy faith, towards which they are much inclined.

I have already said how I went 107 leagues in a straight line from west to east along the coast of the island Juana, and as a result of that voyage I can say that this island is larger than England and Scotland together; for, beyond these 107 leagues, there remain to the westward two provinces where I have not been, one of which they call *Auau*,[12] and there the people are born with tails. Those provinces cannot have a length of less than 50 or 60 leagues, as I could understand from those Indians whom I retain and who know all the islands. The other, *Española*, in circuit is greater than all Spain, from *Colunya* by the coast to *Fuenterauia* in Vizcaya, since I went along one side 188 great leagues in a straight line from west to east.[13] It is a desirable land and, once seen, is never to be relinquished; and in it, although of all I have taken possession for their Highnesses and all are more richly supplied than I know or could tell, I hold them all for their Highnesses, which they may dispose of as absolutely as of the realms of Castile. In this *Española*, in the most convenient

[12] Thus in the Spanish folio, *Avan* in the Spanish quarto, *Anan* in the Latin translation. What Columbus probably meant was Avan, the native name of a Cuban region which gave its name to Havana. Tailed men was one of the most popular yarns of Sir John Mandeville. Columbus and his men frequently inquired about such creatures and were "yessed" by the Indians, who probably thought they were talking about monkeys.

[13] I.e., from Collioure, a port in the Gulf of Lyons that then belonged to Aragon, around the entire Spanish Peninsula to Fuenterrabia, the frontier town on the Bay of Biscay. Like his other estimates of land distances, this was greatly exaggerated.

place and in the best district for the gold mines and for every trade both with this continent and with that over there belonging to the *Gran Can*[Grand Khan], where there will be great trade and profit, I have taken possession of a large town to which I gave the name *La Villa de Nauidad,* and in it I have built a fort and defenses, which already, at this moment, will be all complete, and I have left in it enough people for such a purpose, with arms and artillery and provisions for more than a year, and a *fusta,*[14] and a master of the sea in all arts [15] to build others; and great friendship with the king of that land, to such an extent that he took pride in calling me and treating me as brother; and even if he were to change his mind and offer insult to these people, neither he nor his know the use of arms and they go naked, as I have already said, and are the most timid people in the world, so that merely the people whom I have left there could destroy all that land; and the island is without danger for their persons, if they know how to behave themselves.[16]

In all these islands, it appears, all the men are content with one woman, but to their *Maioral,* or king, they give up to twenty. It appears to me that the women work more than the men. I have been unable to learn whether they hold private property, but it appeared true to me that all took a share in anything that one had, especially in victuals.

In these islands I have so far found no human monstrosities, as many expected; [17] on the contrary, among all these people good looks are esteemed; [18] nor are they Negroes, as in Guinea, but with flowing hair, and they are not born where there is excessive force in the solar rays; it is true that the sun there has great

[14] See note 11 above.

[15] This man must have been either Antonio de Cuéllar, carpenter of *Santa María,* or Alonso de Morales, who was *Niña's* "chips."

[16] A pretty big if! As we have seen, they didn't; some killed each other and the rest were finished off by Caonabó.

[17] See above, note 12.

[18] *Mas antes es toda gente de muy lindo acatamiento.* The meaning is somewhat obscure; the Latin translator of the Letter thought that Columbus meant that the people were reverential.

strength, although it is distant from the Equator 26 degrees.[19] In these islands, where there are high mountains, the cold this winter was strong, but they endure it through habit and with the help of food which they eat with many and excessively hot spices. Thus I have neither found monsters nor had report of any, except in an island [20] which is the second at the entrance to the Indies, which is inhabited by a people who are regarded in all the islands as very ferocious and who eat human flesh; they have many canoes with which they range all the islands of India and pillage and take as much as they can; they are no more malformed than the others, except that they have the custom of wearing their hair long like women, and they use bows and arrows of the same stems of cane with a little piece of wood at the tip for want of iron, which they have not. They are ferocious toward these other people, who are exceeding great cowards, but I make no more account of them than of the rest. These are those who have intercourse with the women of *Matremonio*,[21] which is the first island met on the way from Spain to the Indies, in which there is not one man. These women use no feminine exercises, but bows and arrows of cane, like the abovesaid; and they arm and cover themselves with plates of copper, of which they have plenty. In another island, which they assure me is larger than *Española*, the people have no hair.[22] In this there is countless gold, and from it and from the other islands I bring with me Indios [23] as evidence.

[19] *Viente e seis,* a radical revision downward of the Admiral's two inaccurate calculations that the north coast of Cuba was in lat. 42° N and that of Hispaniola 34° N. Actually 21° and 20° are correct.

[20] At this point the Latin edition of the Letter introduces the name of this island, Charis. That, or Caire, was the Carib name for Dominica. Note that the Admiral's captive Indians had given him the position of this island and told him about the Caribs.

[21] Thus in both Spanish editions, *Mateunin* in the Latin edition, *Matinino* in Columbus's Journal. This was the island afterwards colonized by the French and named Martinique.

[22] What island the Admiral's informants meant by that of the bald natives can only be guessed.

[23] The first appearance in print of this name that Columbus gave to the natives of America.

In conclusion, to speak only of that which has been accomplished on this voyage, which was so hurried, their Highnesses can see that I shall give them as much gold as they want if their Highnesses will render me a little help; besides spice and cotton, as much as their Highnesses shall command; and gum mastic, as much as they shall order shipped, and which, up to now, has been found only in Greece, in the island of Chios, and the Seignory [24] sells it for what it pleases; and aloe wood, as much as they shall order shipped, and slaves, as many as they shall order, who will be idolaters.[25] And I believe that I have found rhubarb and cinnamon, and I shall find a thousand other things of value, which the people whom I have left there will have discovered, for I have not delayed anywhere, provided the wind allowed me to sail, except in the town of Navidad, where I stayed [to have it] secured and well seated. And the truth is I should have done much more if the ships had served me as the occasion required.[26]

This is sufficient. And the eternal God, Our Lord, Who gives to all those who walk in His way victory over things which appear impossible, and this was notably one.[27] For although men have talked or have written of these lands, all was conjecture, without getting a look at it, but amounted only to this, that those who heard for the most part listened and judged it more a fable than that there was anything in it, however small.[28]

So, since our Redeemer has given this victory to our most illustrious King and Queen, and to their famous realms, in so great a matter, for this all Christendom ought to feel joyful and make great celebrations and give solemn thanks to the Holy Trinity with many solemn prayers for the great exaltation which it will have, in the turning of so many peoples to our holy faith, and afterwards for material benefits, since not only Spain but all Chris-

---

[24] The government of Genoa. Columbus as a young man had made a voyage or two to Chios.

[25] I.e., the slave trade is legitimate if Christians are not the victims.

[26] An oblique reference to *Pinta's* leaving him. It will be observed that Columbus says nothing about losing his flagship.

[27] There is no verb to this sentence in either Spanish edition; the Latin ones have interpolated several pious ejaculations.

[28] He probably had in mind the *Book of Ser Marco Polo*, which most of the learned in Europe regarded as fabulous.

tians will hence have refreshment and profit. This is exactly what has been done,[29] though in brief.

Done in the caravel, off the Canary Islands,[30] on the fifteenth of February, year 1493.

At your service.

THE ADMIRAL

Additional Note,[31] Which Came within the Letter

After having written this, and being in the Sea of Castile, there rose up on me so great a wind south and southwest,[32] that I was obliged to ease the ships.[33] But I ran here today into this port of Lisbon, which was the greatest wonder in the world, and whence I decided to write to their Highnesses. In all the Indies I have always found weather as in May; I went thither in 33 days and would have returned in 28 but for these tempests which detained me 23 days, beating about in this sea. Here all the seafarers say that never has there been so bad a winter or so many losses of ships.

Done on the fourteenth [34] day of March.

This letter *Colom* sent to the Keeper of the Privy Purse [35] about the islands discovered in the Indies. Contained in another for their Highnesses.

[29] *Segun el fecho*, a legal term meaning literally, "executed."

[30] So in both Spanish editions; doubtless a misprint, as *Niña* was already off Santa Maria of the Azores on the fifteenth, and Columbus knew perfectly well that he had been in Santa Maria before he sent the letter off.

[31] *Anima* (modern *nema*), a paper wrapped around a letter after its conclusion, and to which the seal was affixed.

[32] *Sueste*, a misprint for *sudoeste*, as may be seen from the Journal.

[33] Plural in both Spanish editions.

[34] *Quatorze*. A misprint for *quatro*.

[35] This official was Luis de Santangel, Columbus's friend.

Index

Index